INDIAN PRAIRIE PUBLIC LIBRARY DISTRICT

3 1946 00581 2604

MAR 1 9 2015

THE PROJECT MANAGEMENT COACH

Jill Dann

D1247404

The Teach Yourself series has been trusted around the world for over 60 years. It has helped millions of people improve their skills and achieve their goals. This new 'Coach' series is created especially for people who want to focus proactively on a specific workplace skill and to get a clear result at the end of it. Whereas many business books help you talk the talk, the Coach will help you walk the walk.

I acknowledge the kind support of my dear husband, Derek Dann, who becomes like a 'golf widower' every time I start writing another book. He is a great proofreader and sounding board. Sandie Pinches, Fiona Willmott and Dr Cathie Palmer Woodward once again helped me to scope the outline of each chapter and to reorganize the order of chapters. Kevin McKee helped me with the chapters on influencing – I was a student of his many years ago, useful learning that has remained with me to this day. Thank you to all friends, family, workmates and clients who continue to support us and enrich our lives.

I dedicate this workbook to the many practitioners I have had the pleasure of working with since running my first project in 1979 as a WRNS Officer IT. I thought that, once I left the military, the battles would be over; however, being an agent of change has marshalled all my tactical planning skills in introducing change to more than 55 organizations in the UK, Europe, USA, Australia and New Zealand. I dedicate this book also to my darling sister, Lesley, who left us too soon in June 2012.

Teach Yourself®

THE PROJECT MANAGEMENT COACH
Jill Dann

INDIAN PRAIRIE PUBLIC LIBRARY
401 Plainfield Rd.
Darien, IL 60561

First published in Great Britain in 2014 by Hodder & Stoughton. An Hachette UK company.

First published in US in 2014 by The McGraw-Hill Companies, Inc.

Copyright © Jill Dann 2014

The right of Jill Dann to be identified as the Author of the Work has been asserted by her in accordance with the Copyright, Designs and Patents Act 1988.

Database right Hodder & Stoughton (makers)

The Teach Yourself name is a registered trademark of Hachette UK.

All rights reserved. No part of this publication may be reproduced, stored in a retrieval system or transmitted in any form or by any means, electronic, mechanical, photocopying, recording or otherwise, without the prior written permission of the publisher, or as expressly permitted by law, or under terms agreed with the appropriate reprographic rights organization. Enquiries concerning reproduction outside the scope of the above should be sent to the Rights Department, Hodder & Stoughton, at the address below.

You must not circulate this book in any other binding or cover and you must impose this same condition on any acquirer.

British Library Cataloguing in Publication Data: a catalogue record for this title is available from the British Library.

Library of Congress Catalog Card Number: on file.

10 9 8 7 6 5 4 3 2 1

The publisher has used its best endeavours to ensure that any website addresses referred to in this book are correct and active at the time of going to press. However, the publisher and the author have no responsibility for the websites and can make no guarantee that a site will remain live or that the content will remain relevant, decent or appropriate.

The publisher has made every effort to mark as such all words which it believes to be trademarks. The publisher should also like to make it clear that the presence of a word in the book, whether marked or unmarked, in no way affects its legal status as a trademark.

Every reasonable effort has been made by the publisher to trace the copyright holders of material in this book. Any errors or omissions should be notified in writing to the publisher, who will endeavour to rectify the situation for any reprints and future editions.

Typeset by Cenveo® Publisher Services.

Printed and bound in Great Britain by CPI Group (UK) Ltd, Croydon CR0 4YY.

Hodder & Stoughton policy is to use papers that are natural, renewable and recyclable products and made from wood grown in sustainable forests. The logging and manufacturing processes are expected to conform to the environmental regulations of the country of origin.

Hodder & Stoughton Ltd

338 Euston Road

London NW1 3BH

www.hodder.co.uk

CONTENTS

MEET THE COACH

Jill Dann is a Chartered Fellow of the BCS, an examiner in Project Management, an acknowledged contributor to the Association of Project Managers' Body of Knowledge, and a PRINCE2 ® and MSP ® Practitioner. She has lectured at Henley Business School, writes for Ashridge Business School, and has written seven books for Hodder.

Jill wanted to write this book because she felt that too many project managers, especially in their first few major projects, focused on hard skills such as scheduling and budgeting, at the expense of soft skills such as stakeholder management. Jill's research interviewing practitioners indicated that there was a clear gap in the market for a book looking at both the technical and the personal perspectives on project management.

HOW TO USE THIS BOOK

 OUTCOMES FROM THIS INTRODUCTION

- Understand the nature and characteristics of projects, which allow us to set ourselves the smallest unique challenges to previously unimaginable questions.

- Grasp the increasing scope and scale of projects.

- Understand the reason this workbook was commissioned, the structure that underpins it, and the coaching approach used in the chapters, which utilizes triple-loop learning.

- Learn some creative techniques that, with practice, will help you see your work with fresh eyes.

Twenty-five per cent of the globe's gross product is spent on projects (approximately £10, or $16.4, trillion), motivation enough for gaining better insight into project management. With £250 billion spent on projects annually in the UK alone, there are 1.5 to 2 million people practising project, programme or portfolio management as employees, contractors or consultants. According to my interviews with senior managers, portfolio, programme and project managers (PMs), the many books on project management methods and lifecycles have insufficient guidance on the soft (but testing) skills associated with change.

THE NATURE OF A PROJECT

The nature of a project can be tested and described by the following:

- A project can be about anything that we want to do or to produce.

- A project is a one-off event; it gets initiated, builds or transforms something, and disappears, leaving behind the outcome of the work.

- Theoretically, a project is unique because no two projects are alike; even if the same method is being used to create something, the personalities of people and their agendas will dynamically change the shaping of the outcome.

- A project does not go on for ever; it is not a business-as-usual operation. At its end point, the outputs of the project work should be handed over to day-to-day operations. A project creates something specified that should be completed by a given deadline.

- A project sets up a construction or development capability, ramps up resources of different types, and applies their skills to finish the item sequentially or in whatever feasible combination they can be utilized. The resources are then rolled off the project, their output tested as defined in the quality policy, both throughout and at the end.

- Projects are all about change, large, small, mandatory, necessary and 'nice to have'. They create things that are new and usually replace some legacy system, business process, regulatory practice or law.

- Projects define what they are going to deliver and this may be a tangible thing or an intangible change of state that has to be made measurable. For example, constructing a new customer centre with all the systems, facilities and furniture that go in the building is very tangible. However, changing the community spirit in an economically depressed region necessitates the invention of identifiable outcomes that evidence when you have succeeded.

- If, during the scoping of a project, it becomes evident that it is not a unique process, it is simply defining a rare process occurring infrequently; it is not, however, a project.

- A project usually generates know-how, knowledge and intellectual property that become artefacts of business value. The permanent organization must be alert to the possibility that the project can generate knowledge and skills. Human Resources (HR) should consider capturing the experience of the human capital involved, especially if individuals are to leave the organization, perhaps once they have been rolled off the team if it is not feasible to do this while they are working on the project.

- Projects have the potential to add to the body of knowledge of the human race and may advance our species; they therefore deserve our respect and our best efforts.

⚇ COACHING SESSION 1

How does your project measure up against the previously described criteria?

_____

_____

_____

_____

_____

_____

_____

THE INCREASING SCOPE AND SCALE OF PROJECTS

The need for projects is increasing in terms of number, scope and scale – for example 'big data' projects. Gartner, the world's foremost information technology research company, describes 'big data' as follows: 'Big data are high volume, high velocity, and/or high variety information assets that require new forms of processing.' It is not a new thing that people want an answer to complex questions that requires enormous volumes of real time or curated data sets. For example, in the 1970s I worked on projects as a Royal Navy IT Officer where customers asked me how the sea-bottom topography and the water column attributes of the entire continental shelf surrounding Britain could be established so decisions could be made about defence strategies. This information had never previously been collected in one place in three-dimensional, electronic form. It was estimated that it would have taken 50 years to survey the entire continental shelf and less than a few hours before any one area's data changed as a result of climate, tide and other planetary forces. In past decades, mainstream computing has not had the processing power necessary to search and collect big data sets.

In research terms, big data comprises information resources so large they exceed the capability of software and other tools to analyse them; thus new approaches, tools and methods are required. We can now ask ourselves previously unthinkable complex questions and muster bodies of knowledge from multiple disciplines.

Social scientists are developing initiatives to curate and analyse big data such as retail data, banking information, transport data and administrative data. In other sciences, the Large Hadron Collider illustrates that so many events are recorded that evidence can be found of *extremely rare* events producing 15 million gigabytes of data annually. This data is analysed collaboratively by a grid comprising more than 140 data centres spread over 35 countries.

A new frontier of competitive differentiation is large-scale data gathering and analytics (e.g. Google, Amazon, Netflix). Organizations and companies in a range of industries (e.g. pharmaceuticals, retail telecommunications, financial products and insurance) are progressing big data strategies using novel strategic approaches. By pursuing relevance and usability, we have enabled ourselves to capture the requirements of a system and to make options increasingly viable in terms of the balance between business value and technical risk.

CEOs face challenges that can prevent big data initiatives from taking root. Depending on the likely action of competitors, the high priorities in existing portfolios of projects and how this impacts strategic priorities, programmes and initiatives may predicate the need for these to be finished first.

Historically, focus groups have been used to assess customer interest but, nowadays, executives ask their data specialists to find those insights using new tools (which can handle large volumes of data and analyse complex questions). In analysing sales numbers, website behaviour, sensor data and social sentiment (e.g. opinions, natural language analysis and contextual polarity), a richer feedback on customer buying behaviour can be gleaned.

COACHING SESSION 2

Reflecting on the examples given above, what applications and collaborations can you think of for your own business?

THE REASON WHY THIS WORKBOOK WAS COMMISSIONED

'Human change isn't something we do, it's everything we do.'

(Burlton 2001)

I interviewed a broad scope of people about interpersonal and intrapersonal skills, stakeholder engagement, influencing strategies and the other topics covered in this workbook. These people held roles such as CIO, General Manager, Portfolio Manager, Programme Director, Commercial Manager and Project Manager. Interestingly, there was a great deal of passion about the potential utility of such a book by all of those interviewed. The consistent response was: 'The skills identified are much needed yet poorly covered.' Among the areas that concerned them were:

- the reassurance provided to stakeholders by greater perception, shrewdness and subtle influence in workplace management
- the importance of practising techniques that can reduce stress at work
- the sheer day-to-day angst caused by deficiency in political savvy
- the need to become more skilled at a personal level and in a manner that is under your control
- the need for a collaborative and supportive relationship with a sponsor (specifically important for all 'change agents', whether at organizational, executive, portfolio, programme or project level).

It did not seem to matter how high or low an individual worked in an organization – concerns were repeatedly about the same topics. These so-called **soft skills** have only recently been added to professional institutes' bodies of knowledge, so it is feasible that there is a gap in the market for practical help in this area.

I consider all of the roles mentioned so far to be 'agents of change'. In addition, I recognize the significant contribution made by HR as a function in transforming organizations. For ease of use throughout the chapters, therefore, the term **change agent** or **project manager** (PM) is used as a blanket term to describe the typical reader, as it is impractical to use all of the possible titles involved in managing change.

THE STRUCTURE OF THIS WORKBOOK

This book is not a management text but uses a coaching approach in a workbook format; you do the thinking, the research and the tailoring of suggested techniques. The degree of utility of the subject matter varies with your background, experience and context. Assessments are provided where appropriate with advice.

For additional templates and supplementary tools, go to: http://www.consultationltd.com/PMCoach, where you can also book a mentoring session with the author for your project, or email jilldann@jilldann.co.uk

You will find the following features in each chapter:

✔ LEARNING OUTCOMES

Each chapter starts with bullet points detailing the main outcomes of the chapter.

COMMENTARY

Each chapter contains commentary or background text in sections giving context or information followed by an exercise for direct application by you at work on project management challenges. The headings of background text in blocks will be appropriate to the chapter's subject and each block will be followed by a coaching session (exercise).

💬 COACHING SESSION

While exercises apply to everyday project management challenges, if you are between project assignments the coaching sessions can act as a contribution to improvement initiatives regarding governance practices, policies, toolsets, methods and behavioural skills. The coaching sessions include:

- workplace exercises using the discoveries made from completing a self-assessment
- illustrative charts and tables for you to complete
- checklists or tick lists
- forms and worksheets (for recording or challenging beliefs/thoughts)
- specific direction to achieve an outcome by studying other resources such as methodologies, bodies of knowledge, research papers and standards
- questions whose aim is to guide your learning.

🖱 ONLINE RESOURCE

These boxes will contain complementary online resources and coaching sessions for you to download free of charge and make use of.

NEXT STEPS

At the end of each chapter you will find a summary of what you have learned and what you have done in the chapter, as well as what comes next.

TAKEAWAYS

At the end of each chapter, there is a 'write-in' section of three or four questions for you to reflect on what you have learned from the chapter.

You have the choice of tuning into a specific topic that is giving you the greatest challenge at work, or of working through the whole book. It's up to you.

Useful project management books and reference materials for any models or concepts used can be found online at www.TYCoachbooks.com/ProjectManagement.

LEARNING DESIGN

The coaching sessions ask questions at each of the three levels of learning, following the model of **triple-loop learning** (first postulated by Garratt (1986) and Swieringa and Wierdsma (1992)):

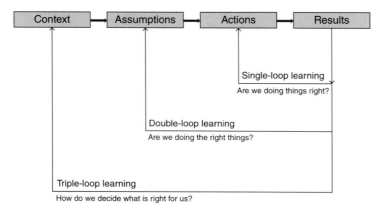

Figure 0.1 Triple-loop learning

- **Are we doing things right?** Single-loop learning is about making minor adjustments to current practices based on a linear perspective of the current process and what is wrong with it. It asks what is wrong and how to correct it.

It seeks actions to correct issues and assumes that action and results are closely associated and, hence, feasible. Single-loop learning is essentially about solving problems in a task-focused manner.

- **Are we doing the right things?** Double-loop learning is more than just problem solving – for example, it looks at the policies and products of the organization that may be at odds with each other. This is tackled in double-loop learning by permitting their objective evaluation without politics and prejudice acting as delays or blockers. It uses more creative and evaluative thinking styles. Double-loop learning asks why something is wrong and how a recurrence can be prevented.

- **How do we decide what is right for us?** Changes in the environment need to be responded to, potentially radically, by questioning the business model. It is important that an organization challenges assumptions it holds about itself and does not stagnate.

There are many theories on learning and some of these are given in the reference list downloadable from www.TYCoachbooks.com/ ProjectManagement. Triple-loop learning suggests an openness to challenge by asking why you exist as you do; it is the main prescription for organizational innovation, quantum leaps and breakthroughs. It involves organizational creativity coupled with knowledge creation. It is about reframing and contextualizing observed behaviours and constructing entirely new ways of succeeding, as appropriate. It may require a whole repurposing of a project.

If you are an experienced PM, you may not realize that what you know is of relevance until you are placed in a situation where that wisdom is called upon:

- **Explicit knowledge** This is knowledge and expertise that is easy to express and to pass on to other people. Knowledge becomes wisdom when it has been put repeatedly to use and provides the holder with anecdotal evidence of reliability, enabling him or her to prevent a bad outcome.

- **Tacit knowledge** Experts in their field are often immersed in work using contextual expertise that is not easy for one person to pass on to another. Tacit knowledge is insight that arrives at the moment it is needed – a valuable know-how that might be lost unless ways of passing it on are found. Tacit wisdom can be drawn out by specific interviewing techniques. Experts find it difficult to verbalize or structure the content because they do not consciously 'know what they know'.

- **Wisdom** This is the capacity to realize what is of value in life for oneself and others, such as knowledge, understanding and technological know-how. The philosopher Bertrand Russell defined it as 'the capacity to take account of all the important factors in a problem and to attach to each its due weight'. This workbook is intended to make you more wise or savvy in your role.

You may have access to explicit knowledge through written-down processes, methods, lifecycles, policies and techniques, either online or on paper.

In the organizational context, the role of tacit knowledge is critical in the learning process; it is essentially the interaction between tacit and explicit knowledge. Thus, the intent in structuring the background text and accompanying coaching sessions is for you to be able to apply triple-loop learning in progressing your role, project and organization. Triple-loop learning is about adaption for survival, by, for example:

■ questioning existing techniques and systems by asking *where* the organization should stand in the marketplace or in public service

■ exploring *how* to be creative and innovative to succeed in the marketplace or in public service.

We will explore this further in later chapters.

Coaching session 3 will enable you to assess your appetite and willingness to shift your point of view – how ready are you for triple-loop learning? Try this out to test your ability to take a different approach.

CREATIVE THINKING TECHNIQUES

Let go of any preconceived thinking about project management methods, lifecycles and approaches. These methods are *complementary* to this workbook's activities and goals; it is a question of 'and', not 'or':

■ Open your mind to new possibilities.

■ Drop your PM experience-based assumptions.

■ Defer forming a judgement and concluding your thinking.

■ Explore divergent concepts before forming conclusions.

■ See your own portfolio, programme or project with fresh eyes and enjoy it!

🗨🗨 COACHING SESSION 3

Imagine you are going to sell your car (or bicycle). Use another object if you wish but follow the same approach. Get a clipboard and pen and walk around your car making observations about its design, condition and features as if you have never seen the car before.

You might consider the possibility of taking a structured approach to this:

- **Exterior**

    - Exterior design, condition and features

    - *Exterior facilities:* petrol filler and cap, windscreen wipers, lights, parking sensors, wing mirrors, roof rack or tow bar

    - Locks, alarm and other safety features such as roll bar

    - Windscreen and other windows

    - Bumpers

    - *Tyres:* design specification, suitability for road conditions, wear condition, known repairs, age, estimated time remaining, pressure settings

- **Interior:**

    - Interior design, condition and features

    - *Interior facilities:* steering wheel, main dashboard displays and controls, drinks holders, glove box (with or without lock), other switches (seat adjustment, own window, door handle), radio, music system, satellite navigation, mobile phone connectivity, armrests and trays or pockets, ashtrays, cigarette lighter, map pockets, air vents, handles and grips, seats and headrests, legroom, seat belts, seat conversion or removal, child seat safety features

    - *The boot or trunk:* spare wheel, toolset, luggage capacity, storage, flexibility of space, anchorage points

    - *The engine compartment:* capacity, design, condition, maintenance and features

    - The fuel (petrol, diesel, dual, other) tank capacity

However, there is also the possibility of taking a completely different approach from the logical – for example, an appeal to the senses:

- *Colour impact and cultural compatibility:* For example, the Chinese like black gloss with red leather interior or trim as these are their lucky colours in Chinese culture. However, what would a complete stranger from a different background feel about it? What is your association with the colour of your car?

- *The smell:* When you smell the exterior and interior of the car, what memories does it evoke? It could be going for picnics with your parents as a child, or cleaning the car with your dad (polish, leather), or taking your first date home…

- *The feel:* How does the car feel – are the doors weighty in your hands when they swing shut; is the paint smooth and glossy; does it look impressive and do people want to be seen in it?

You have been generating perceptions and impressions of your car or another familiar object. Have you managed to avoid judging ideas and kept on allowing new ideas to flow? You should keep generating ideas and perceptions for as long as possible.

It is a challenge to stop your brain's desire to flip-flop between generating ideas and converging thoughts into evaluation of the ideas. It is important that you keep divergent thinking and convergent thinking as two separate stages, so you must defer judgement of your own ideas and those of other people until the generation stage is exhausted.

Our mind hates ambiguity, so it seeks to resolve the uncertainty; it looks for patterns in order to form impressions to evaluate the object as to how it affects our chances of survival in our current environment. Our brain centres match patterns so that a new experience can be fitted into an existing mental framework.

A paradigm shift occurs when you are able to perceive that your existing framework is unsuitable and that a new one must be created or another one adopted and integrated.

PERCEPTION AND REALITY

COACHING SESSION 4

The following diagram is a flat set of lines and a dot.

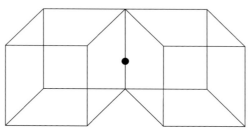

Figure 0.2 Our mind plays tricks on us

Stare at the black dot and let your mind roam free.

The diagram is just lines on a page; however, your mind fills in the gaps so that you perceive things that are not there. What our brains perceive and what is a reality can be two different things.

You may notice that your perception of the orientation of the lines changes into 3D objects and that more than one viewpoint can be taken on those objects.

Using this insight, reconsider the change that you are charged with implementing. You could break it down logically, as demonstrated in the car exercise using internal and external decomposition. Equally, however, you could take the approach that appeals to the senses, instead of the logical mind. Change has equivalent emotive associations and an outstanding change agent recognizes this, tunes into it and uses the information gained to their advantage.

Thus, creative thinking can extend the range of ideas available to us at all stages of the change process, not just in scope definition and seeking agreement on the way forward. Perception and reality can be different because of the way our minds work. You may be distorting the state your project is in or missing the gaps. Looking through a different lens may offer a better perspective.

COACH'S TIP

Practise!

You need to hone your skills and demonstrate that they are improving. By the end of this workbook, you will see your own portfolio, programme or project with fresh eyes and enjoy it! We are talking about your new *behaviour*, not just a list of new *tasks*.

NEXT STEPS

Every chapter has one main theme that you need to grasp. This means that you should have tested it out in your own reality, the 'here and now' of your everyday life. You may have to 'be it', not just 'do it', so it will require willingness to experiment and evaluate the degree of success of any exercise that you implement. It's about behaviour.

The next chapter examines motivation under pressure and how this affects your role as a PM leading a team of people towards a goal.

 **TAKEAWAYS**

How much of your organization's annual turnover is made up of change programmes and projects? What percentage does that represent?

_____

_____

_____

_____

_____

_____

_____

_____

_____

How well does your organization develop the interpersonal, intrapersonal and leadership skills of those involved in leading and managing change?

_____

_____

_____

_____

_____

_____

_____

_____

_____

_____

How does the triple-loop learning model compare with how your organization develops itself and manages learning at work?

_____

_____

_____

_____

_____

_____

_____

What completely different approach from the logical can you take to scoping your project in order to be open to a different world view?

_____

_____

_____

_____

_____

_____

_____

_____

MOTIVATION UNDER PRESSURE

 OUTCOMES FOR THIS CHAPTER

- Understand the definition of the human resource approach to employee motivation.
- Use a diagnostic template for assessing your self-motivation.
- Fill in a checklist for what employers value in their employees.
- Understand different theories of motivation and their relevance to change programmes.
- Complete reflective exercises on change priorities and discover how to apply them to your team.
- Complete a worksheet to diagnose and introduce measures to reduce stress.

Releasing employees' full potential and instilling a responsibility-oriented culture remains the best way to compete in a 'do more with less' business climate. Motivating yourself and others under pressure is a vital aspect without which PMs are unlikely to succeed. This chapter provides the means to assess the project manager's self-motivation and aids their job of inspiring team members to be motivated positively. As we will see, this is more of a craft than pure science.

A HUMAN RESOURCE APPROACH TO EMPLOYEE MOTIVATION

Motivation is the set of forces that cause people to choose certain behaviours among the many alternatives open to them. Motivation is having enthusiasm and drive, the incentive and inspiration to do a good day's work on a project and the impetus to help it reach its goals.

The human resource approach guides most thinking about motivation today; it assumes that people want to contribute to organizational effectiveness and are able to make valuable contributions. The organization's responsibility is to create a work environment and climate that makes full use of people's potential; this applies as much to temporary workers such as project team members and suppliers as it does to permanent employees.

The assumption that work is inherently unpleasant for most people and that earnings are more important than the nature of the job is today considered old-fashioned. One school of thought emphasizes the role of social processes in organizations and assumes that a sense of belonging and the need to feel useful are more important than money in motivating employees:

- Managers and organizations need to be skilled in how to create and maintain an empowered, motivated workforce – one dedicated to constant improvement in terms of quality, output, sales and customer satisfaction.

- Employees need to recognize that being motivated is about being enthusiastic and determined to succeed on one's own account. Changing your mood and stance is possible because we are all made with a capacity for mood control.

- PMs need to know how to assess the motivation of individuals before deciding what adjustments need to be made to their role and workload.

 ONLINE RESOURCE

Diagnostic test for self-motivation

Download and complete the self-motivation diagnostic. This will help you reach a view of how motivated you are at the moment.

www.TYCoachbooks.com/ProjectManagement

The self-assessment contains feedback for different ranges of score. You can use it on your own and with your team members as part of a team-building workshop.

 COACH'S TIP

Self-motivation

To have this competency, you would:

- be driven to improve or meet high standards
- demonstrate commitment in all your relationships
- look for the opportunity first, not the problem
- show persistence in pursuing goals and determination to overcome barriers or setbacks.

WHAT EMPLOYERS VALUE

Project team members need to know 'what good looks like' in your eyes. While employers value and pay for specific behaviours at work in each role, an employee chooses certain behaviours based on what they perceive to be the value of the outcome of that behaviour; this may be a subconscious choice.

Employers value a person who:

- delivers the behaviour at work that the employer wants to pay for ☐
- takes the initiative ☐
- brings discretionary effort to work voluntarily ☐
- adds value to the organization and the work they are selected for every day ☐
- brings knowledge and expertise to the organization and transfers it before they leave ☐
- keeps their personal problems away from the workplace as much as is feasible ☐
- when they walk in the room, lifts the spirits of the people around them ☐
- makes the effort to understand the diversity among colleagues and how differences can be utilized to strengthen work flow and outcomes ☐
- is generally positive about continuing to learn and helping to improve things ☐
- communicates well and makes an effort to comply with expected standards. ☐

A team member who meets all of the above criteria would be deemed an actively engaged employee – that is, a well-motivated person, someone who does what is needed and expected of them for the remuneration and rewards agreed or through a sense of loyalty to the organization employing them.

 ONLINE RESOURCE

Valued employees checklist

Download and complete the template checklist.

You can edit the checklist to add additional criteria suitable for your change programme or aspects of your culture, vision, mission and values. Use this as an exercise if you have a team at the present moment and develop it into a questionnaire when recruiting additional team members. You can use it on your own or with your team members as part of a team-building workshop. The important things is that you recognize that you are 'crafting' skills – therefore, be willing to experiment, evaluate and objectively measure what works and, equally, what does not work.

www.TYCoachbooks.com/ProjectManagement

MODELS OF MOTIVATION

As in any management topic, there are rafts of theories on the subject of motivation. Some are hugely beneficial to our gaining a good, practical understanding of the subject:

- Maslow's Hierarchy of Needs
- Herzberg's Hygiene Theory
- McGregor's 'Theory X' and 'Theory Y'
- Victor Vroom's Expectancy Theory (simplified form).

Others have contributed to the debate, of course, but here we'll concentrate on the most popular. Let's think about how we can use each of these to benefit our own project.

Maslow's Hierarchy of Needs

The broad recognition afforded to Maslow's theory is due to its being easily understood. Maslow presented no empirical data to support his theory and subsequent research has been unable to validate his thinking. Regardless of this, many experienced change agents find applying his thinking to project environments to be of benefit in anticipating and preventing motivation or dissatisfaction issues.

Maslow proposed that people's needs could be described as a hierarchy, shown in Figure 1.1:

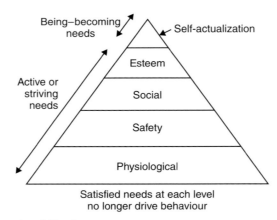

Figure 1.1 Maslow's Hierarchy of Needs

- **Physiological** Physiological needs include those required for sustaining human life such as food, water, warmth, shelter and so on. Maslow was of the opinion that, until these physiological needs have been substantially met, other motivational factors have little, if any, impact.

- **Safety** This is the need to feel free from threat or danger, physical or emotional harm. Imagine the impact of rumours that 50 per cent of the workforce are to be made redundant once your project delivers. What might that do to your team and to your motivation?

- **Social** This is our need for company, affection and human interaction; the need for acceptance as you are, for a sense of belonging, to have friends, and to be liked or valued emotionally.

- **Esteem** This concerns our need for recognition, for being held in high regard by others, and for a feeling of accomplishment and of 'a job well done'. Without our high self-esteem, we are likely to suffer from poor motivation.

- **Self-actualization** This is the highest order of human need and the most mature, and concerns our drive and determination to achieve our full potential. Maslow suggested that this human is also associated with altruistic behaviour – where we want to 'pay back' into our communities, social groups and society at large.

Remember, motivation acts as an inner engine that makes us get up each morning and get on with things we do well. While the levels are typically depicted as a hierarchy, each need does not exist in isolation to one another. Each need exists in varying proportions according to the degree of satisfaction of those needs, as illustrated in Figure 1.2:

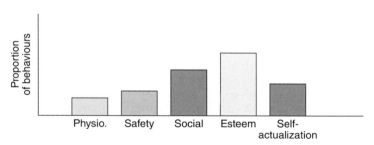

Figure 1.2 Maslow's Hierarchy of Needs in proportion

As each of these needs is substantially satisfied, the next need becomes more dominant as a driver or motivator. External factors, such as a recession, can force you back down the hierarchy again, as can internal factors.

COACH'S TIP

Moving down the hierarchy

If someone loses their job, their safety needs would increase in importance, while higher needs such as self-actualization would decrease. This same person would therefore automatically adjust their basic needs to take account of this changed position.

In general, when recruiting, a company will look for factors relating to a person's esteem needs – that is, their ability to work harder or better. Yet the worker may not yet have reached the esteem level or it may represent a relatively low level in proportion to their other needs such as physiological, safety and social needs. The difference between your expectations of what will motivate an employee and what needs they are seeking to have satisfied at that time may be very different.

This is an important consideration to bear in mind when dealing with project team members.

Herzberg's Hygiene Theory

Herzberg postulated a two-factor theory in which he identified 'hygiene factors' (things that make employees dissatisfied) and 'motivation factors' (things that provide positive impetus). He suggested that within organizations intrinsic factors are related to motivators whereas extrinsic factors are associated with dissatisfaction. Whereas Maslow was *not* concerned solely with the working environment, Herzberg's model is explicitly so defined:

- **Dis-satisfiers** Removal of job security, good pay, a good supervisor or pleasant working conditions causes dissatisfaction.

- **Motivators** Reinforcement or enhancement of your sense of worth or importance (i.e. recognition), your sense of being valued by the organization, praise for a job well done, and a sense of achievement drive positive motivation.

Consider the working conditions and environment in your current place of employment. If the conditions are good, this becomes the expected standard and is neutral as a motivator; whereas, if conditions are poor, they will almost certainly be a demotivator (a source of dissatisfaction).

For projects, the dis-satisfiers and the motivators arguably have a bigger impact because the accommodation provided is frequently temporary, less pleasant and less secure. In the instance where there is a demographic of employees who are always working on projects, who must hot-desk and endure other factors reinforcing their sense of 'not belonging' or being valued, you should expect demotivated workers.

The following coaching session invites you to consider the Maslow and Herzberg models of motivation and what they can tell you about your current team members' state of motivation.

⊋⊋ COACHING SESSION 5

Evaluate impacts on motivation

Having studied both the Maslow and Herzberg models as concepts intended to illuminate how and why people become dissatisfied or become inspired and positively motivated, think about how this relates to your project and its people. Consider the members of your team and colleagues – it could be a peer, someone more junior or senior to you – and the impact your project may have on their hygiene factors and Hierarchy of Needs. (For example, one stage of your project may change their job description, role or grade/status, promotion prospects, while another stage may change their office accommodation.)

1. What might be acting as dis-satisfiers and what else is a motivator?

_____

_____

_____

_____

_____

_____

2. Which need might be next for them, in your opinion?

_____

_____

_____

_____

_____

_____

_____

3. Do they understand the Hierarchy of Needs and how it modifies their behaviour at different project stages?

_____

_____

_____

_____

_____

_____

_____

4. Do they know what drives them on?

_____

_____

_____

_____

_____

_____

_____

McGregor's 'Theory X' and 'Theory Y'

McGregor suggested that people in organizations could be managed in one of two ways depending on their attitude to work:

- **'Theory X'** people are those who work because they have to, those who do not like work and who will do as little as possible or avoid it altogether; they will need a 'carrot and stick' management style and will resist taking on new responsibilities. Usually, they are more concerned with security needs than with esteem needs such as achievement and ambition.

- **'Theory Y'** people find work stimulating and energizing; they want to be a part of a successful organization and will do whatever they can to help it achieve that. They are imaginative and creative, and accept and seek out responsibility and new challenges to stretch their capabilities and expand their knowledge and skills. They are actively engaged employees who will bring discretionary effort and external know-how into their work.

However, there is no suggestion here that people's outlook regarding work is necessarily reflected in their attitude towards life in general; feasibly, we can have totally different attitudes and approaches to work and pleasure.

Consider the PM's responsibilities and approach to introducing change. In such situations, people will often resist change because of:

- individual attitudes, inertia, preferences and personal characteristics, commitment to the old way of doing things, a general reluctance to change

- difficulty in identifying 'ownership' and identifying the need for change:

    - Who requires the change and why?

    - Who will champion each change?

- professional or intellectual disagreement with the new approach and/or threatened loss of knowledge and skills

- fear that they may not be able to cope with new processes, policies and procedures or that these may not work or will create extra work

- social and political factors – changes in work groups and relationships, transference of power, responsibility or influence.

Now think about the nature of change and how sensitive it may be to people with differing attitudes (Theory X or Y). Consider:

- changes to the user requirement – new staff, restructuring the organization, customer requirements, different user stories and user journeys

- changes in the business – competitor activity, financial pressures, market forces, shared services, alliances, mergers and acquisitions

- changes in the outside world – government legislation, global competitive forces

- changes required because of imperfections in the original plans

- changes required because of errors in implementing the original plans – incorrect design assumptions and off-specifications.

COACHING SESSION 6

McGregor categories

Reflect on the descriptions of resistance and the nature of change given above in relation to your own team. You could use this exercise as a team-building exercise.

1. Think about some of your work colleagues and decide which McGregor category you would place them in.

_____

_____

_____

_____

_____

_____

_____

_____

_____

_____

2. If some of them are Theory X types, what could you do to help them realize their full potential?

_____

_____

_____

_____

_____

_____

_____

_____

_____

_____

_____

_____

Vroom's Expectancy Theory

The chart below describes Vroom's theory in simplified form:

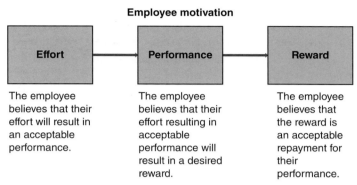

Figure 1.3 A simplified model of Vroom's Expectancy Theory

Vroom's theory suggests that motivation is based on how much we want something and how likely we think we are to get it. The individual is satisfied if the rewards are equitable relative to the effort expended and to the level of performance attained.

PMs, therefore, should first determine the outcomes each team member is likely to want. Then they should decide what kinds and levels of performance are needed to meet project targets or goals, making sure that the desired levels of performance are attainable. PMs then need to ensure that desired project stage or work package outcomes and the desired performance or quality are linked. The amount of effort required by the individual must be available according to the project plan using a resource-levelling process after determining the critical path for the project.

STRESS CAUSED BY WORKING IN CHANGE PROGRAMMES

Stress is:

- 'A gap between the demands you perceive are being made on you and your perceived resources to meet those demands.'
- 'Pressure or tension causing physical and/or mental strain leading to a temporary or permanent incapacity.'

Stress is a 'dis-ease'; people are not at ease when they suffer stress.

When considering potential stress in high-intensity change programmes, recognizing signs of extreme stress is essential whether with colleagues or stakeholders. It is helpful to be aware of what happens to people physiologically and psychologically when they work like this. Individuals may have what is required technically to carry out activities but the climate at work may not be conducive to them delivering at their best for extended periods.

If employees are not demonstrating expected productive behaviour, you as their PM must find out why not, so that you both have the chance to improve matters. A team member's performance is typically influenced by motivation, ability and the work environment. Some deficiencies can be addressed by providing training or altering the environment; motivational problems are not as easily addressed. There may be reasons such as the person is suffering from stress; it is possible that you can change something that allows them to perform at their best. Three motivational interventions are:

1. **Behaviour modification** This is a technique for applying reinforcement of desired behaviours such as in a project setting.

2. **The modified work week** This can be any work schedule that does not conform to a traditional eight-hours-a-day, five-days-a-week design. Some alternatives include the compressed workweek, flexible work schedule, working at home and job sharing.

3. **Work redesign** Changing the nature of people's jobs can be used as a motivational technique. Examples include alternatives to task allocation, job specialization, job rotation, job enlargement, job enrichment and so on.

 ONLINE RESOURCE

Stress diagnosis worksheet

Download the stress diagnosis worksheet to help you diagnose sources of stress, reduce stress and manage individuals who are failing to thrive in current circumstances. If the suggested interventions do not fit your project, edit the downloadable template to suit your own project's context.

www.TYCoachbooks.com/ProjectManagement

 NEXT STEPS

In this chapter we have met some of the most popular theories relating to (self-)motivation and you have carried out a series of reflective exercises to help you relate these theories to your day-to-day experience of project management. The next two chapters cover influencing skills and strategies that build on your understanding of self-motivation so that you become adept at managing people at all levels and roles. The chapters also distinguish between appropriately assertive behaviour and aggressive or coercive behaviour.

👍 TAKEAWAYS

What is your greatest challenge in terms of self-motivation?

_____

_____

_____

_____

_____

_____

In order to manage others more effectively and have a positively motivated team, which skills do you need to improve? Seek feedback from colleagues if you are willing to do so.

_____

_____

_____

_____

_____

_____

Have you team members who require an intervention due to their level of performance, motivation, discretionary effort or dissatisfaction with rewards? Identify specifically what changes need to be made.

_____

_____

_____

_____

_____

_____

Which motivational model is the most applicable to the project and team members and why?

_____

_____

_____

_____

_____

_____

Is your understanding of this chapter sufficient to see how it relates to your project lifecycle and team management? (The next chapter gives you more background on influencing skills.)

_____

_____

_____

_____

_____

_____

_____

INFLUENCING SKILLS

2

- Gain a practical understanding of influence by analysing and comparing situations in which you have been an effective influencer and another where you were less successful.

- Carry out a self-assessment to establish your current capability as an influencer and identify areas for improvement.

- Understand what productive behaviours look like and their benefits.

- Assess and contextualize your assertiveness and responsiveness skills in the context of your change agent role.

- Experiment with a positive influence process, putting individual influencing skills into practice and reflecting on the degrees of success.

Frequently, PMs are not delegated sufficient authority over resources or the customer relationship; other managers may 'own' the money, people, development environments or facilities required for the project outputs and outcomes. In addition, resistance is frequently encountered during production and delivery because the workforce takes issue with the planned changes. PMs need to practise influencing skills in a balanced fashion so that they are effective, appearing neither overly pushy nor passive.

WHAT ARE EFFECTIVE INFLUENCING SKILLS?

Influencing is an active process whereby one person or a group modifies the attitudes or behaviour of another person or group by adapting their own behaviour and communication style in order to gain agreement and commitment to ideas or to action.

Influencing is not about being pushy; someone who agrees to an action when faced with a pushy individual is likely to resent their behaviour and renege on the agreement later. Effective influencing skills are quite the opposite; they are a balance of responsive and assertive behaviours that together engender true influence. Other people feel respected and that their needs are understood, and are persuaded by your logical reasoning. If you lack *position* power (delegated from above through legitimate line authority), then you can generate *personal* power (becoming the 'go to' person or expert) by becoming a skilled influencer and project expert.

This chapter identifies specific skills that need to be honed if you are to exert influence. You may be already adept at some skills, but a PM needs to be proficient at balancing planning, agility, flexibility, responsiveness and assertiveness skills to be an effective influencer. Chapter 3 will build on this and will explain key influencing strategies; if you grasp these skills, they will facilitate you taking your negotiating and persuading skills to the next level. Both skills and strategies are utilized in the chapters on the end-to-end communications plan, mobilizing change, stakeholder management, political savvy, improving the customer journey, creating powerful relationships with sponsors; thus, they are a foundation for other activities. The skills are self-assessed and you will work through exercises for each of them and in combination.

SELF-ASSESSMENT

The following self-assessment exercises (Coaching sessions 7, 8 and 9) enable you to identify development needs in your role. You can select those that appeal or may apply, but you should perhaps adapt them to your own situation. The first (Coaching session 7) is a situation analysis (as illustrated in Figure 2.1), enabling

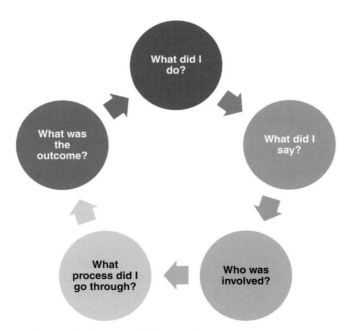

Figure 2.1 Situation analysis cycle (© Jill Dann FBCS, CITP)

you to compare a successful influencing situation with one where you did not triumph. You will then go on to document those discoveries and insights in Coaching sessions 8 and 9. If discoveries and insights continue to elude you after you have tried different situations and analysed them, try sharing them with a trusted individual who may be able to help you reflect on your influencing skills.

Influencing skills tend to be more subtle than persuading or negotiating skills. Utilizing the right skills will enable you to affect people's thinking without them realizing, because, used well, influencing skills affect other people subconsciously. Influencing skills are intriguing to learn and effective to use. Understanding them not only makes us better communicators; they are also worth investing time in because they enable us to spot manipulative people trying to influence us detrimentally.

COACHING SESSION 7

Self-assessment: situation analysis

Think of a situation where you were successfully influential and another where you were unsuccessful, then analyse what happened by documenting the results in the following table.

Situation analysis	Description/Response
Think of a situation where you were **successfully influential** and analyse what happened. Ask yourself:	Situation:
What did I do?	
What did I say?	

Situation analysis	Description/Response
Who was involved?	
What process did I go through?	
What was the outcome?	
Think of another situation where you were **not influential** and again analyse it. Ask yourself:	Situation:
What did I do?	
What did I say?	
Who was involved?	
What process did I go through?	
What was the outcome?	

COACHING SESSION 8

Self-assessment: learning outcomes from situation analysis

What can you learn from this situation analysis in terms of your influencing strengths and weaknesses? List your observations and insights.

Learning point	Outcome observations, insights and actions
1	
2	
3	
4	
5	
6	

COACHING SESSION 9

Self-assessment: what would you do differently?

At the end of your thinking through this self-assessment cycle relate 'What did I do?' to 'What was the outcome?' Draw inferences about what you could do differently next time.

Outcome	What I could do differently

WHY ARE INFLUENCING SKILLS IMPORTANT TO CHANGE AGENTS?

Any manager has to get the right work done by others in the right way for the right purposes. Change agents have less time to do this in a project than in business-as-usual, so there is more pressure to get decisions quickly from those in power – change agents, in short, need to build a power base through influencing others. If authority is not delegated from above to you over others, then you can develop productive behaviours and gain recognized 'personal power', as illustrated in Figure 2.2.

Productive	Unproductive
Assertive (I WIN) Expressing want Rewards and penalties Giving feedback Logical persuasion	**Aggressive (YOU LOSE)** Interrogating Patronizing Showing contempt Attacking
Responsive (YOU WIN) Active listening & enquiring Expressing appreciation & support Sharing Learning/Disclosure Finding common ground Visioning	**Passive (I LOSE)** Accommodating Self put-downs Self-pitying Avoiding

Personal power is gained from below

Figure 2.2 Productive behaviours in personal power (© Developed by Cole-McKee from the work of Situation Management Systems, USA and Malcolm E. Shaw, *Assertive-Responsive Management* (Reading, MA: Addison-Wesley, 1979))

The quadrants in Figure 2.2 illustrate the diverse sets of behaviours that have either beneficial or detrimental impact on the person you are trying to influence. As seen on the left-hand side of the matrix, productive behaviours are appropriate to long-term relationships. The best mix of behaviours is a balance of assertive and responsive behaviours (you will be invited to complete self-assessments in respect of these later in this chapter). This means that the best way to encourage productive team behaviours is to demonstrate them and become a role model.

I once worked as consultant alongside a team managing an organization-wide transformation programme. Towards the end of my 18-month spell I asked the team to complete a 360-degree appraisal of my influencing skills and my influencing strategies. The results suggested that I had excellent skills on both sides but that I was using assertiveness only to about 75 per cent of capacity, yet my responsiveness skills were around 90 per cent. The message was that I should, unashamedly, be more assertive because I was already making people feel good using my responsiveness. By ramping up the assertiveness, I would have more impact, but still without appearing pushy. In other words, I could achieve a better balance between assertiveness and responsiveness.

Unproductive behaviours will not achieve any desirable outcomes, but you need to know how to handle them should they arise; indeed, you may need to exercise self-control and self-discipline under trying circumstances. People respond to the pressures involved in the environment of a project or programme in diverse ways. Even the most enlightened in normal conditions can behave against their norms in these circumstances.

If you observe any of the unproductive behaviours on the right-hand side of Figure 2.2, you need to identify how this behaviour has come about. While the individual is responsible for behaving in an aggressive or a passive way (especially if it is habitual rather than incidental), the organization is responsible for not intervening in this behavioural pattern. In both instances, passive or aggressive, responsibility is being transferred or unevenly attributed for whatever is going on. These individuals will benefit from your leadership example in modelling productive behaviours and in receiving your support in making necessary changes to their own attitudes and behaviour. You will benefit from feedback on your own performance in doing so.

It will come as no surprise that change management requires all levels of manager to be excellent at:

- planning
- strategy, policies and initiatives
- portfolio, programme or project
- flexibility/adaptability
- modelling the ability to change for others.

KEY INFLUENCING SKILLS AND COMPETENCIES

A planning capability is amply covered in a host of books on methods, bodies of knowledge, training programmes and qualifications. However, effective influencing also requires the following qualities, skills or competencies:

- **patience** – a real and essential virtue for agents of change
- **the ability to accept ambiguity** while individuals are internalizing the impact of a change on their role, work or life. In other words, you need to allow people time to explore the future, their options and the nature of change for them. This requires the agent of change to suspend any personal requirement to conclude change quickly, though only for a reasonable time.

- **self-awareness** – the emotional intelligence required to see yourself as others see you and to identify the roots of strong emotions in past experiences
- **awareness of the feelings and motivations of others** – the empathy with and appreciation for other people's emotions and rights
- **'pull' skills** – active listening and other responsiveness skills (detailed below)
- **'push' skills** – assertiveness and other 'push' skills (detailed below).

The main influencing skills, 'push' and 'pull' skills, are described in the following sections. Both push and pull strategies have merits and it would be a mistake to suggest that either one is more important than the other. Study the descriptions and diagrams and complete the self-assessments in the following sections. Remember these capabilities are built on in later chapters, so obtaining a good grasp of them now will be beneficial in maximizing what you get out of the other subjects.

PULL SKILLS

The responsive, or 'pull', behaviours are shown in the bottom left-hand corner of Figure 2.2. They are important because of the subtle effect they have on other people's self-esteem. They feel heard, understood, valued, consulted, trusted and inspired. Those exhibiting such behaviours pull information out of people and then check that the understanding is correct. They do not push their intentions on to others without considering others' needs. The following pull skills will be described in more detail (along with self-assessments) below:

- **Active listening and enquiring** This requires self-discipline in listening to others, and self-control in body language while listening.

- **Expressing appreciation and support** This shows others that they are liked and valued for their contribution. The person with this skill will seek others out and offer help when it is needed.

- **Sharing learning and disclosure** The person with this skill gives others facts or feelings about the situation to help them make effective decisions or operate more effectively.

- **Finding common ground** The person with this skill looks for areas of mutual interest and knowledge and helps others to work more harmoniously.

- **Visioning** The person with this skill uses words and images to describe the future in ways that help others to see possibilities and to view the future positively.

Active listening and enquiring skills

We hear sounds with our ears but we listen to people with our minds and pay attention to the meaning. People demonstrate that they are actively listening by using open body language, reflecting what they have heard, checking understanding, summarizing, and using open questions to gain insight. Collectively, this capability is termed 'active listening and enquiring'. For ease of assessment, each of the components are explained here separately.

Active listening is an important skill for effective influencing and one that many individuals find challenging. Not only does the influencer have to understand their own demeanour and impact on others, but they must also be aware of the need to quieten their inner voice and hear the other person. Key here are maintaining well-balanced eye contact and expressing an interest in the discussion. Typically, this is done by the use of interjections ('indeed', 'mmm', 'ah', 'yes', etc.) or facial expressions (smiles, head nods, eyebrow movements) or small gestures indicating the absorption of what is being said by others.

COACHING SESSION 10

Self-assessment: active listening

Read the preceding description of active listening and identify which of the skills you demonstrate. How do you rate your listening capability from 20 for 'outstanding' down to zero for 'very poor'? Ask trusted colleagues for their view if you like, too. List all their observations and insights.

Learning point	Outcome observations, insights and actions
Score out of 20	=

Enquiring is used to gather further information from listening to someone to gain a richer understanding of the issue or emotions involved. Figure 2.3 illustrates a questioning technique using open questions followed by probing, reflecting and making statements that repeat the phrases used by the other person to summarize and show understanding. It is often referred to as 'funnelling' because the technique focuses the person down from a lack of clarity or ambiguity to specific information or a conclusion.

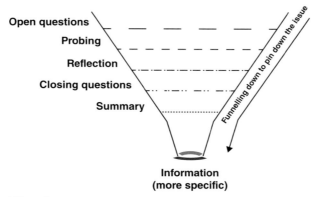

Figure 2.3 Enquiring skills using the 'questioning funnel'

The steps are:

- skilful use of **open questioning** (what, where, why, when, how, who)
- asking questions in order to get a **shared and full understanding** of the issue
- using open (what, where, when, why, how, how much, who) and probing questions in order to **check the accuracy of your understanding**. For example:
    - 'What do you attribute as the root cause of the incident?'
    - 'What was your motivation at the time?'
    - 'What methods did you apply to...?'
    - 'What is your recollection of events and how they could have been managed differently?'
    - 'Does the following summary accurately reflect your perception of what occurred and what can you learn from it?'
- careful use of some **closed questions** so that you are able to reach a conclusion jointly.

COACHING SESSION 11

Self-assessment: enquiring

Study the preceding description of enquiring skills and Figure 2.3. Repeat the process in the previous coaching session, rating your questioning and summarizing capability from 20 for 'outstanding' down to zero for 'very poor'. List your observations and insights.

Learning point	Outcome observations, insights and actions
Score out of 20	=

Expressing appreciation and support

This behaviour:

- shows others that they are liked and valued for their contribution
- engenders a sense of being positively affirmed
- seeks others out and volunteers practical and emotional help when it is needed
- helps to build 'personal power' and shows warmth and enthusiasm for other people.

COACHING SESSION 12

Self-assessment: expressing appreciation and support

Study the above description. How do you rate your ability to express appreciation and engender a sense of mutual support? Give specific examples of praising others with specific evaluative feedback and instances where you have successfully supported others at appropriate times. List your observations and insights.

Learning point	Outcome observations, insights and actions
Score out of 20	=

Sharing learning and disclosure

As a leader, it is powerful to share examples from your own life as it makes you more approachable and credible in leading change. It also gives others facts and feelings about a situation, thus helping them to make effective decisions or to operate more effectively.

By using examples from your own learning such as when you have been vulnerable or self-doubting or have transgressed, you demonstrate that you trust the person and are equally human. This can act as a powerful metaphor for another person's dilemma, aiding exploration of the underlying issues.

ΩΩ COACHING SESSION 13

Self-assessment: sharing learning and disclosure

Study the description of sharing learning and disclosure skills. How do you rate your ability to share your learning and engender a sense of mutual trust by disclosing moments of truth in your own life? List your observations and insights.

Learning point	Outcome observations, insights and actions
Score out of 20	=

Finding common ground

This behaviour fosters dialogue that explores another's experience and opinions for mutual benefit in order to increase rapport and trust. Dialogue does not, however, include debate about what someone has just said, as illustrated in Figure 2.4. Instead, each person voices what they really think about a chosen issue and are listened to by everyone else without interruption or comment. Each person respects the integrity of the others and any assumptions or judgement is suspended for the duration of the dialogue.

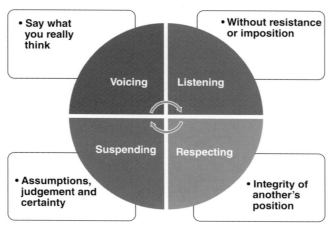

Figure 2.4 Dialogue model (*source*: William Isaacs, *Dialogue and the Art of Thinking Together: A Pioneering Approach to Communicating in Business and in Life* (New York: Random House, 2008)

A person exhibiting this behaviour:

- looks for areas of mutual interest and knowledge and helps others to work more harmoniously
- seeks to contextualize another's experience in order to identify points of relevance and focus priorities appropriately to the current circumstance.

COACHING SESSION 14

Self-assessment: finding common ground

Study the description and diagram above. How do you rate your ability to create dialogue, to explore others' experience and opinions, and to establish common areas of interest that could bind you? List your observations and insights.

Learning point	Outcome observations, insights and actions
Score out of 20	=

Visioning

This behaviour uses words, gestures and imagery to describe the future in ways that help others to see the possibilities and to view it positively or from completely different world views. It can include creative visualization techniques such as those commonly used in sports performance coaching.

🗨🗨 COACHING SESSION 15

Self-assessment: visioning

Study the description above. How do you rate your ability to describe the future in ways that help others to see the possibilities? List your observations and insights.

Learning point	Outcome observations, insights and actions
Score out of 20	=

PUSH SKILLS

Assertive behaviours act as the counterbalance to responsive skills, but there are fewer of them.

- A **push influencing** strategy carries conviction and has impact. The following steps are a reasonable example: setting the scene, inviting reactions, summarizing, dealing with objections and agreeing the outcomes.

- A **pull influencing** strategy by comparison involves creating rapport and ease in your company: inviting stakeholders to explore and define the scope of work, prioritizing and contextualizing the results of the scoping, gaining agreement on a joint diagnosis and mobilizing the changes, reviewing results and agreeing the next steps.

The assertive behaviours are illustrated in the bottom left-hand corner of Figure 2.2 above. As in the previous section on pull skills, complete each self-assessment by reading the preceding description and identifying which of the skills you demonstrate. How do you rate your capability – from 25 for 'outstanding' down to zero for 'very poor'? The score is 25 this time to make a hundred in total for the four skills.

Expressing want

This behaviour involves:

- telling others what you want (without justifying it but not without reason)
- telling others what you expect from them with a clear bottom line
- stating the required standards unambiguously and with clarity.

⧉⧉ COACHING SESSION 16

Self-assessment: expressing want

Study the description above. How do you rate your ability to be assertive about what you need and expect from others? List your observations and insights.

Learning point	Outcome observations, insights and actions
Score out of 25	=

Rewards and penalties

This behaviour involves:

- telling others what they will gain if they co-operate and fulfil your expectations or, if they do not, what they will lose (in this way the consequences of non-compliance are understood)

- offering appropriate incentives or pressures to sway the argument towards your position

- stating your expectations clearly and unambiguously, resulting in a strengthened position.

COACHING SESSION 17

Self-assessment: rewards and penalties

Study the description of rewards and penalties skills. How do you rate your ability to strengthen your position and communicate the consequences of not matching your expectations? List your observations and insights.

Learning point	Outcome observations, insights and actions
Score out of 25	=

Giving feedback

A person with this skill:

- informs another about facts and feelings relating to the impact of their behaviour

- provides observations as to what they can continue to do and addresses attitudes using concrete examples

- identifies what should change in order for them to be more effective.

COACHING SESSION 18

Self-assessment: giving feedback

Study the description above. How do you rate your ability to provide specific, evaluative feedback to a sufficient degree to persuade someone to do things differently? List your observations and insights.

Learning point	Outcome observations, insights and actions
Score out of 25	=

Logical persuasion

A person with this skill:

- presents arguments in a logical and rational way and with conviction
- uses facts and data to back up opinions and to overcome counter-arguments.

💬💬 COACHING SESSION 19

Self-assessment: logical persuasion

Study the above. How do you rate your ability to convince others and counter their arguments? List your observations and insights.

Learning point	Outcome observations, insights and actions
Score out of 25	=

YOUR PUSH/PULL BALANCE

You have now finished your self-assessment for both assertive and responsive skills. The four assertive skills were scored out of 100 in total and therefore account for up to 25 per cent of the total each. The five responsive skills were scored out of 100 in total, and therefore account for up to 20 per cent of the total. Results are best when you get feedback from work colleagues and bosses and any staff that report to you. Most companies should have schemes similar to this to support continuous professional development. Examine your self-assessment scores and, ideally, seek a trusted colleague's opinion on them. Adjust them accordingly.

Now consider how well balanced your assessment is between the two styles (see Figure 2.5).

Figure 2.5 Balance of influencing skills

If you remember from earlier in the chapter, my results were that I had excellent skills on both sides but I was using assertiveness only to about 75 per cent, yet my responsive skills were around 90 per cent. The feedback was that I should give myself permission to be more assertive because that way, by ramping up the push element, I would have more impact without appearing overly assertive.

COACHING SESSION 20

Self-assessment: your push/pull balance

Insert your scores for assertive and responsive behaviours from the previous exercises to find out your own balance of pull and push. Now ask yourself:

1. What is the current balance between your push and pull skills?

_____

_____

_____

_____

2. Are your skills evenly balanced or skewed one way or the other?

_____

_____

_____

_____

Think through the implications of your current balance between the push and pull skills. Are there situations where you did not get the results you needed and could have been more responsive to others?

Equally, reflect on times when you could have been more assertive in a balanced way and achieved a better outcome.

_____

_____

_____

_____

_____

_____

Record your scores and make notes in the space provided in the table.

Influencing skill	Score
Assertive	Push style
Expressing want	
Rewards and penalties	
Giving feedback	
Logical persuasion	
Score total	

Influencing skill	Score
Responsive	Pull style
Active listening and enquiring	
Expressing positive regard and support	
Disclosure	
Finding common ground	
Visioning	
Score total	
Balance =	Score e.g. (75% Assertive/90% Responsive)
Your ratio is:	☐ % / ☐ %
Based on this my development plan is:	What I need to do by when…

In the next chapter, you will have the opportunity to look at influencing strategies and then plan those influencing strategies that are applicable to your project.

PUSH/PULL SKILLS IN A POSITIVE INFLUENCE CYCLE

It is a cliché to say that you have to win the hearts and minds of your project's stakeholders, but neuroscience backs this up with hard evidence about how people communicate deeply with each other in generating trust and achieving agreement. Each stakeholder group will be impacted by change in a unique way, and your role as a change agent is to mobilize that change and help make the changes stick.

The flowchart in Figure 2.6 shows you one kind of cyclical influence process using the push and pull skills, matched with other attributes such as planning and emotional intelligence aimed at mobilizing change to a jointly agreed change agenda.

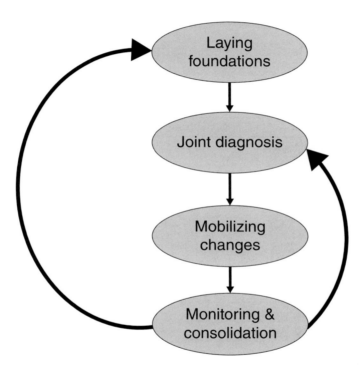

Figure 2.6 Positive influence process (© Cole-McKee Partnership/Hudson Associates)

By using the influencing skills and doing your homework on each stakeholder (covered in Chapter 7), you will:

■ identify how to lay down a good foundation for a relationship with each stakeholder

- create rapport in your interactions and display emotionally intelligent behaviour in all your communications with stakeholders
- be able to craft relevant messages and elicit what is required from stakeholders.

Choose the most relevant methods of delivering messages and creating buy-in that will build your credibility in their eyes and their interest in you. By planning the involvement of stakeholders throughout the project stages, you can create opportunities for monitoring their commitment and consolidate the transition from the start to its finish.

ΩΩ COACHING SESSION 21

Self-assessment: effective influencing through every project stage

Look at Figure 2.6 above, which shows the positive influencing process, and think about how you can be a more effective influence throughout the specific stages of your project.

Project stage	Influencing skills and process
How will your lay down foundations for your project to positively influence key stakeholders?	
Which actions demonstrate your willingness to jointly diagnose the nature of change involved?	

Project stage	Influencing skills and process
Are you at a project stage where you can envisage change being easily mobilized?	
How will you test the appropriateness of your actions – are you doing the right things?	
How will you check progression and productivity?	

GETTING THE RIGHT BALANCE

Let's remind ourselves of the triple-loop learning explained in the Introduction, using it as a prism through which to view your influencing skills and their appropriateness for your project at its current stage:

- *Are we doing things right?* Look at your score for each influencing skill – is there room for improvement or is it optimal?

- *Are we doing the right things?* Assess the balance of your push/pull influencing skills and its impact on the project team at this stage of the project.

- *How do we decide what is right?* In the current market conditions, is doing the project still the right thing? Has the need for it changed?

COACHING SESSION 22

Consolidate your learning

Answer the questions in the following table to consolidate your learning.

Triple-loop learning questions	Answer
What would be the optimal balance for your current role?	
Which actions demonstrate the assertiveness and responsiveness skills required for your role?	
Are you at a project stage where you need to be more assertive or more responsive, or balanced?	
What assumptions are you making about the appropriateness of your actions — are you doing the right things?	

Triple-loop learning questions	Answer
Have previous actions led to the conditions causing current problems?	
Is how you are currently behaving the right response for the project environment and organizational culture?	
Is the project still producing the outputs needed by the business for the current market conditions?	

 ## NEXT STEPS

By studying this chapter, you should have achieved an understanding of your current influencing capability and the importance of achieving an effective balance between your push and pull influencing skills.

Having analysed where you are, you were invited to use a cyclical influence process (as illustrated in Figure 2.6) to plan your own influencing process, working with a colleague as required.

You were then reminded of triple-loop learning (discussed in the Introduction) and encouraged to challenge your assumptions about the appropriateness of your current influencing process in your current situation – skills, balance and context.

The next chapter explains influencing strategies; these will take your negotiating and persuading skills to the next level.

TAKEAWAYS

What is your greatest challenge in being an effective influencer at work?

_____

_____

_____

_____

_____

_____

_____

_____

_____

Which skills do you need to improve and who can help you?

_____

_____

_____

_____

_____

_____

_____

_____

_____

_____

_____

Is there a suitable balance between your push and pull skills? Identify specifically what changes need to be made.

_____

_____

_____

_____

_____

_____

_____

_____

_____

Which skills will be the greatest asset to the particular nature of your project in terms of a positive influence process?

_____

_____

_____

_____

_____

_____

_____

_____

_____

_____

_____

_____

INFLUENCING STRATEGIES

3

✔ OUTCOMES FROM THIS CHAPTER

- Understand the importance of different communication styles to both project performance and to success in your role.
- Grasp the differences and similarities between persuading, influencing and negotiating.
- Know about learning by example by looking at a case study drawn from the education sector.
- Know about the different influencing strategies available to you.
- Assess how well you think you operate as an influencer.

PMs need to appreciate the importance of persuading, influencing and negotiating to both project performance and to success in their role. Being skilled at matching the most appropriate influencing strategy for your particular situation needs to be contextualized in terms of stakeholder engagement and management of allies or opponents.

To exert effective influence in an organization, whether within the entire organization or at divisional, departmental or group level, you need to take its culture into account. A behaviour that may be appropriate at one structural level may be wholly inappropriate at another. Similarly, a strategy that worked well in one organization may not be appropriate to another organization.

Being culturally sensitive is a type of behaviour that is generally valued or considered fitting within an organization. The required behaviour may differ, for example, between people at different levels. Who is perceived to have power in the organization and how they use it is also part of organizational culture.

DIFFERENT SOURCES OF POWER

Traditional hierarchical organizational structures with line managers, senior leadership teams and an executive have split authority into areas of accountability or functions with different delegated limits of authority (usually financial). These areas of authority are, in general:

- **Legitimate authority over others** This induces compliance because others feel that their position in the organization gives them the right to expect to be followed. Explicitly discussing what power you hold tends to make people feel dominated, manipulated or coerced.

- **The ability to reward** The use of rewards such as promotion, bonus levels, foreign travel, pay and recognition encourages compliant behaviour.

- **Status by association** Demonstrable connections with important people to gain favour (or avoid disfavour) raises your status and can impress others.

- **Coercive inducement** This involves the use of punishments or the right to veto to gain compliance.

It may be that the people with the most decision-making authority are doing their job and helping the project along. Alternatively, they may be inexperienced, overly busy or preoccupied elsewhere with matters other than your project. This is where you need to understand the relative importance of each stakeholder group at each stage of the project; this topic will be dealt with in Chapter 5: End-to-end communications planning.

If you do not have a position of power over all the stakeholders, then you need to match your desire to influence them with the time that you have available to do so. However, when it comes to change management, the management of work is organized through a governance process over a management and technical lifecycle of some kind. The common elements are as follows:

- The overall timescale is divided up during a planning phase as befits the unique requirements and nature of the project.

- There may be a technical lifecycle underlying a regular set of managed stages or phases.

- There will be a decomposition of the end deliverables with a definition of interim deliverables mapped to each stage or phase.

- There may be 'gates' or other milestones where a go/no go decision is made based on information reported up to senior managers from a PM.

Therefore, a manager responsible for change (project, programme, portfolio or strategy) does not have a fixed area of responsibility or authority regarding anything other than a time-limited basis (a stage's duration or phase). Instead of being allocated an annual budget, the finances are justified in a business case with a cost/benefit profile aligned to the project's stages. Generally, PMs do not have a pot of money to move around at their discretion to pay for different purchases. The project's accounting tends to be for resources consumed in a project stage, a situation unlike that found in business-as-usual operations.

THE IMPORTANCE OF COMMUNICATION STYLES TO PROJECT PERFORMANCE

While it is an assumption that your authority and power as a PM will not be as strong as you would ideally like it to be, a savvy change agent will acquire or utilize communication skills reinforced with one, or a combination, of the influencing strategies described later in this chapter.

With hard work and research, and by being diligent in getting to know the organizational structure and the key stakeholders, you can become influential even if your official delegated limits of authority are not what you would have wished for in taking up your role. (This happens to people regardless of whether they are self-employed, consultant, interim or permanent members of the workforce.)

Being an effective influencer involves developing responsive and assertive influencing *skills* AND having the ability to wield whichever influencing *strategy* matches the respective interests of each stakeholder group. This is how you learn to cope should you not have official influence and power over customers to do what you, as the PM, need to them to do.

Honing skills and being willing to experiment with new behaviours feels risky and takes courage. However, this is the politically savvy route to getting the project or programme on track, complementing standard best-practice methods and toolsets.

Assessing the people involved helps you to consider the whole influence relationship rather than just a tactic for a specific meeting or event (e.g. 'show and tell', focus group session, workshop). In a people-centred culture, the wise would concentrate on the use of 'personal power' over line authority where appropriate.

People with 'personal power' are the 'go to' person for a particular programme; they are the one 'in the know'. A person with 'personal power' is:

- **a project expert** – they influence others to comply out of respect for their expertise, skill or knowledge in a particular area;

- **a reliable source of information** – they influence others through the possession of or access to information that others value and which they proactively generate and research so as to keep it fresh and relevant;

- **a recommended referent** – they influence others by being very useful to know because they are admired for their impact and willingness to share know-how and can be identified with on a personal level.

All positive influencing strategies require adaptive and agile behaviour from you in matching your behaviour to the situation.

COACHING SESSION 23

Communication style review

Take some time to review your communication style by filling in the following forms, reflecting on the questions posed and recording your thoughts and insights.

Exercise	Answers
STYLE REVIEW Reflect back on your typical approach to influencing:	
Would you say your style was more 'telling' or 'selling'?	
Ask others for feedback on your typical approach to influencing.	
CURRENT SITUATION Think about a current influencing situation you are facing:	
Write down what you consider to be the other parties' current views on the issue.	
What are the advantages and disadvantages of your proposal from their perspective?	

What does this tell you about the approach you should adopt and process you should go through?	
INFLUENCING OTHERS Think about the people you have to influence:	
What types of people do you find easiest to influence and what types of people do you experience difficulties with?	
Does this tell you anything about yourself and your style?	
WORK WITH OTHERS Do you enlist the help of others by:	
Asking for feedback on your approach to influencing?	
Working through your approach with someone else prior to the influencing situation?	
Role-playing the situation, especially if you anticipate difficulties?	

WATCH OTHERS Observe others when they are influencing — especially those you admire:	
Identify the strategies and skills they use and try to incorporate them into your own influencing approach.	
EXAMINE YOURSELF Think about situations outside work when you have to influence others:	
What strategies and skills do you use?	
Which of these can be applied at work as well?	
BEING INFLUENCED Think about a time when you were influenced:	
What strategies and skills worked on you?	
What can you learn from this?	

While people usually have one style as a preferred approach, you need to be flexible because alternative strategies may suit different individuals on the same issue. You need to identify which of them will be more effective on those people on whom you rely for support. Several strategies may be used in combination.

THE IMPORTANCE OF PERSUADING, CHALLENGING AND NEGOTIATING

We all have a natural communication style and we may acquire the ability during our upbringing and education to add a few more to our toolkit. However, in the fast-paced world of change projects, the person with the most agile behaviour tends to be the biggest influencer because they can adapt to changing circumstances and craft the right message for each audience.

To engage people's hearts and minds, you must immerse them in *experiences* (not lectures) that give life to the reasons for change and illuminate employees' understanding of the impact it has on them.

COACHING SESSION 24

Self-assessment: persuading, challenging and negotiating

Complete the following diagnostic self-assessment on persuading, challenging and negotiating.

Communication style	Reflection on your style
PERSUADING SKILLS	
Persuasion follows a rational/conscious process of getting others to agree with you.	
The questioning funnel (Figure 2.3) – discovering and using the other party's perspective and logic to identify specific agreement.	

Communication style	Reflection on your style
Using probing as a persuasive tool.	
Mirroring language and order, using the right words in the right sequence.	
Wearing another hat, switching their perspective to one that helps your case.	
Tailoring what you say to their logic to highlight flaws in their argument.	
CHALLENGING SKILLS	
At times, people need to proactively 'challenge' or 'test' another party positively.	

Communication style	Reflection on your style
Are you good at balancing challenge and support? How do you respond to challenging situations? Do you avoid argument or conflict?	
What do you understand as the differences between assertive and responsive behaviour and aggressive and passive behaviour (see Coaching sessions 28 and 29)?	
Identify how and when understanding your rights and quoting them has been useful to you.	
Identify how and why understanding body language has been useful to you.	
Identify how and when controlling your emotions made you influential.	
Identify which challenging techniques you have used and why.	
Identify how diffusing anger and resolving conflict have been useful to you.	

Communication style	Reflection on your style
Identify examples of you acting as arbiter.	
NEGOTIATING SKILLS (If persuading and challenging skills haven't been enough to enable you to reach a desired outcome, negotiating is the next step.)	
How does negotiating relate to persuading and challenging?	
Are you a natural negotiator or a reluctant one?	
What are the component parts of negotiating?	
Identify how and why increasing your bargaining power helped in a situation.	

Communication style	Reflection on your style
Explain how you show understanding of the other party's needs and position.	
What negotiating ploys and gambits do you utilize?	
How do you resist the negotiating ploys and gambits of others?	
Explain which body language makes the right impression as a negotiator.	
How do you rate your ability to read other people's non-verbal communication?	

THE DIFFERENT INFLUENCING STRATEGIES AVAILABLE TO YOU

The following table gives a description of seven different influencing strategies. The difference between each strategy is highlighted by the mix of assertiveness and responsiveness behaviours required to carry them off effectively. Some take longer than others to take effect.

Strategy	Application	Prerequisites	Key behaviour	Potential pitfall
Friendliness	Any situation where trust, openness and a strong personal relationship are required.	• Time • Contact with the person/people you wish to influence • Positive feelings towards them	All the responsive behaviours, especially 'expressing positive regard and support'. Some 'logical persuasion' or 'expressing want'.	This is a strategy requiring time. The liking expressed must be genuine for it to be a positive strategy.
Empowerment	Where you are in a leadership role and need others to take more responsibility.	• Knowing the overall direction to be taken • Time • Patience	Primarily responsive behaviours, especially 'active listening and enquiring'. Also 'expressing want' or 'logical persuasion' on overall direction.	Takes plenty of time to work; needs real commitment from the leader.
Vision/ Inspiration	Adaptable to any situation where long-term enthusiasm or commitment is required.	• A clear personal vision • Energy and enthusiasm • Creativity to blend your vision with the visions of others	Primarily responsive behaviours, especially 'finding common ground' and 'visioning'. Some 'expressing wants' to show your own commitment.	Can be seen as insubstantial unless backed by other strategies.
Building alliances	Ideal when support is needed to achieve your objective.	• The right contacts • Common interests with potential allies	Could demand the full range of behaviours. 'Finding common ground' usually the key behaviour.	Allies will expect reciprocal support so there is a cost.
Expertise/Data	A powerful strategy where data/evidence can be brought to bear conclusively on an issue.	• Access to significant data/evidence • Being seen as an authority/expert (or having access to one)	'Logical persuasion' is the central behaviour. It must be balanced by responsive behaviours, notably 'active listening/enquiring'.	Can founder if resistance is at the level of emotions or values.
Bargaining	At its best when securing support or neutralizing opposition on specific issues.	• Usable incentives and pressures	'Expressing want' and 'rewards and penalties' in assertive. 'Active listening/enquiring' and 'finding common ground' in responsive.	Success is contingent on your continuing to provide incentives and pressures.
Position power	Where you have an acute need for things to happen quickly, or where commitment is not needed from others.	• You must be seen as having the right to make the demand/request (or be backed by someone who has that right)	Primarily assertive behaviours, particularly 'expressing want'. Disclosure can sometimes make this strategy more palatable.	Likely to result in compliance, not commitment.

COACHING SESSION 25

Reflect on your own experience as an influencer

Which of the influencing strategies do you see as one of your strengths? Make notes in the space provided in the following table. Which strategy is the one required for your project at the current time? Can you identify any stage or phase in the project's life when this will change and you will need to deploy different skills and strategies to remain an effective influencer?

Position power

Using position power alone reduces the chances of an actively engaged workforce. While position power is useful for making things happen quickly, it relies heavily on the four push skills of expressing want, rewards and penalties, feedback and logical persuasion. Using your position within the organization to influence others and relying solely on delegated line authority will usually result in compliance but not necessarily long-term commitment. If you rely solely on these assertive behaviours with little counterbalancing responsive behaviours, you will earn grudging compliance to directives. People will be inclined to leave their discretionary effort and capability at home.

Your reflection on the relevance of this strategy for you

Bargaining

This is a good fall-back strategy when others have failed. Bargaining is useful for securing support or neutralizing opposition on specific issues (say, access to resources). Since its success depends on having something to trade and the use of incentives, you will need to understand others' requirements as fully as possible. Knowing their bottom line is essential so that you can negotiate the best support for your cause. It is usually effective only while the incentives (or disincentives and pressures exerted by you) remain active and available.

Your reflection on the relevance of this strategy for you

_____

_____

_____

_____

_____

_____

_____

_____

_____

_____

_____

_____

_____

_____

_____

_____

_____

_____

Expertise/Data

This will be the strategy most expected to be used in governance of a project (the reporting cycle, toll gates, reviews, permission to proceed to the next stage or phase, project closure and so on). Organizations like this influencing strategy because logic is widely used as a currency in getting decisions. It requires the use of relevant, substantial, appropriately weighted and timely data backed by expert opinion to reinforce what you want to achieve. The evidence and proposals need to be targeted to hit the objective. It may require you to increase your own level of expertise in persuasion, negotiation or gaining support from others. You may need to enrol other specialists in providing expert analyses such as investment profiles, articulating the benefit spectrum, hardening up intangible benefits, countering irrational arguments and resistance to change.

Your reflection on the relevance of this strategy for you

_____

_____

_____

_____

_____

_____

_____

_____

_____

_____

_____

_____

_____

_____

_____

Building alliances

This involves finding common interests with potential supporters. You need to identify and make contact with potential allies and find issues that you can agree on which you may lobby together to get a decision pushed through. The common interest may be expediting something, removing barriers or opposition. Similarly, it could be combining skills to create a more comprehensive capability as an alliance, and branding as such.

Develop a mutual understanding of how you will support one another. For example, by formalizing an alliance, you may develop a shared services strategy over waste management, energy supply, training, computer services and consumables. Thus, purchasing utilities and other products or services together saves on all your budgets. Suppliers are often willing to give considerable discounts to alliances for a reliable bulk purchase with no credit issues. Suppliers may give you preferential terms if you make life easier or cheaper for them to work with you, for example simplifying payments, providing premises on-site, or allowing people to work from a cheaper geographical location.

Your reflection on the relevance of this strategy for you

Vision/Inspiration

The key here is to develop a shared vision that appeals strongly at an emotional level. You must demonstrate genuine enthusiasm for others' aspirations and connect these to your own so that others buy into it as their own (part) creation. Vision can be presented logically but this will only be convincing for a short time with some emotional rapport.

There are specific techniques that can help such as creative visualization (which is an NLP technique). This is where we can place ourselves mentally in another time and place under different circumstances and use this to identify our response and reactions. Using our imagination, we can simulate another existence.

To inspire others to make a transformational change, you need to accept that they may be sensing a threat to their survival or identity. Inspiring others to make a change means creating a new place of safety in which they can operate successfully and be valued.

Your reflection on the relevance of this strategy for you

Empowerment

Empowerment involves you doing the following:

- Providing clear and overall direction to someone without controlling the detail of content or process

- Providing access to resources estimated and requested by them

- Showing confidence and trust in others' capabilities

- Listening and showing empathy without removing responsibility

- Being willing to change your own plan based on feedback from them.

Your reflection on the relevance of this strategy for you

_____

_____

_____

_____

_____

_____

_____

_____

_____

_____

_____

_____

_____

_____

_____

_____

_____

_____

Friendliness

The intention of using friendliness as an influencing strategy is that, by building trust and rapport, the other person will accept your suggestions and ideas in a collaborative fashion. Friendliness takes the longest time to work as an effective influencing strategy as you must show consistent warmth, positive regard and practical support. It is one that many people instinctively try when they join an organization because it is has worked for them in school or in community life.

It may be harsh to say that it is the default mode for the politically naive; not everyone in the workplace seeks friendship. Some ambitious and authoritative individuals keep a strong divide between work and home life. Very ambitious individuals may make friends with those who can be useful to them through their connections or control over resources. The behaviour appears friendly but is essentially bargaining or building alliances in disguise.

There is much debate about cross-gender friendship in the workplace. Many men do not expect to make friends with women at work, especially if the woman is their boss. However, men expect their boss to command respect from everyone. According to *Psychology Today*, cross-sex relationships can be very successful as men receive more support in talking through emotional situations from women colleagues than they do from male-only groups. Women get support, humour and a sense of having a 'big brother' watching their back. It may lack the roller-coaster effect that female relationships can bring, however.

In cultures where trust, openness and strong relationships are valued, friendliness is a useful and rewarding strategy for influencing. It must, however, be authentic, congruent and genuine if it is to be successful.

Your reflection on the relevance of this strategy for you

COACHING SESSION 26

Identify a strategy for improvement

Identify one strategy that needs strengthening and improvement given your current situation and culture. Resist solely picking the one that you feel is your weakest influencing strategy as the entire focus of development action planning. Record your selection and planned actions below.

My selected strategy for improvement is:

My action plan is:

COACHING SESSION 27

How well do you think you operate at the moment as an influencer?

If you feel able, using the table below seek feedback as to which is your observed preferred strategy from up to four others who have had the opportunity to see you utilizing your influencing skills and strategies, and generate development actions accordingly.

The more responsive influencing strategies are at the top of the table and the more assertive towards the bottom.

Influencing Strategy	Who				
Friendliness	Self				
	Others				
Empowerment	Self				
	Others				
Vision/Inspiration	Self				
	Others				
Building alliances	Self				
	Others				
Expertise/Data	Self				
	Others				
Bargaining	Self				
	Others				
Position power	Self				
	Others				

COACH'S TIP

Find a mentor

It will be useful if you can seek a mentor inside or outside the organization. Professional institutes frequently have their own mentoring schemes (such as the British Computer Society, the Chartered Institute for IT or the Association of Project Managers).

ONLINE RESOURCE

Case study: influencing skills

Download a case study drawn from the education sector showing how a newly appointed principal was able to turn his college's prospects around by deploying his influencing skills.

www.TYCoachbooks.com/Projectmanagement

NEXT STEPS

In this chapter, you have looked at the seven distinct influencing strategies available to you, each drawing on a mix of the assertive and responsive behavioural skills explained in the previous chapter. Through a series of reflective exercises, you were asked to assess how well you think you operate at the moment as an influencer. You were invited to plan progress by identifying and scheduling actions.

As is the pattern for this workbook, the next chapter, on proactive conflict resolution, draws on the concepts explained in the preceding chapters on motivation, influencing skills and strategies. So far, we have focused on shaping your team and making it productive. However, since conflict and resistance arise all too frequently in projects, programmes and portfolios, it is essential that PMs can identify aggressive and passive behaviour in anyone impacting them and have the skills to counteract any unproductive effect this may have.

TAKEAWAYS

How effective an influencer do you think you are? If you have applied and practised the exercises in this chapter, you and your project should be able to gain the benefits described in the following table by you being an effective influencer. Identify what progress you have made and your plan of action to improve in the space provided.

Benefits of effective influencing strategies	My progress and planned actions
BENEFITS OF IMPROVEMENT TO ME:	
To have greater self-confidence	
To have the ability to involve others and get their commitment	
To have greater levels of respect from others	
To have the ability to manage change	

Benefits of effective influencing strategies	My progress and planned actions
BENEFITS OF IMPROVEMENT TO MY ORGANIZATION:	
Being flexible enough to cope with change	
Being willing and able to delegate more	
Creating higher levels of morale among their own staff	
Having a greater chance of hitting targets by being able to mobilize all the resources within their control	
Building and developing effective work teams	

PROACTIVE CONFLICT RESOLUTION

4

 OUTCOMES FROM THIS CHAPTER

- Learn about conflict resolution and game theory – and understand why attempting to resolve conflict can feel like a game.
- Know how to match your behaviour to the circumstances.
- Predict potential confrontation between parties and take proactive action.
- Use the Responsibility Assignment Matrix to reduce team confrontations and clarify other key parties' responsibilities.
- Understand the emotional roots of conflict.
- Use Belbin team inventories in resource allocation in order to utilize the diversity in the team.

PMs can prevent a good deal of the conflict that commonly arrives on a project by predicting at which point conflict may occur and about what issues. In addition, identifying and using diversity in the team is a fantastic investment in conflict prevention. In this chapter we will explore answers to the question: 'What can I do to increase the quality of relationships and reduce destructive conflict in my project team and stakeholders?' Further, PMs are encouraged to choose their teams and to develop them.

CONFLICT RESOLUTION AND GAME THEORY

The term 'conflict' refers to perceived incompatible differences resulting in some form of opposition, resistance or interference. Whether the differences are real or not, if people perceive that a difference exists, then a state of conflict can ensue.

Certain people argue that some conflict is necessary for the wellbeing of an organization, as in creative dialogue, debate, or research and innovation. Key to achieving the optimal output of group meetings is the use of constructive debate; this uses the emotional intelligence competence of 'constructive discontent'. However, there is a difference between conflict and constructive discontent, since in the latter diverse 'devil's advocate' views of a proposition are taken in order to generate informed discussion.

In Chapter 2 (Figure 2.2) we looked at unproductive and productive behaviours, which included some of the following game theory descriptors. Those attempting to resolve conflict often talk about a result being viewed as:

- **Win-Win** This is achieved when the real issues are confronted; where both parties are happy that the conflict has been resolved after debate.

- **Win-Lose/Lose-Win** Where one party achieves their goals at the expense of another.

- **Lose-Lose** Where nobody gets what they want and will have negative feelings about the encounter.

So it is important to understand as we go through the subject of this chapter, resolving conflict proactively, that victory is in the eye of the beholder. A win-win outcome is a *perception* of how each party views the results. However, for exactly the same economic gain, one party may view the result as a loss while the other perceives it as a win.

This simple principle applies in change projects; the logical argument alone may not be sufficient to win the day, even when you may have to change through external drivers. Stakeholders and other players may choose to play games that hinder, delay or divert the necessary outcome. PMs need to know 'what good looks like', to anticipate types of conflict and situations:

- **Vertical conflict** This is between different levels in the organization affecting the project strategy.

- **Horizontal conflict** This occurs between people, peer groups or PMs working at the same level in the organization and may affect the allocation of human resources, environments, accommodation or facilities.

- **Manager–staff conflict** This is between line management and project personnel, for example between a team leader and a resource owner. The business staff may be stakeholders and this conflict could be partly due to their attitude to the purpose of the project.

Of course, effective managers know that, when forming a team, there has to be a storming stage before people settle down into performing well together. The psychologist Abraham Maslow is quoted as saying: 'If the only tool you have is a hammer, everything else in the world will look strangely like a nail.'

MATCH YOUR BEHAVIOUR TO THE CIRCUMSTANCES

As a PM, you should carefully observe and react appropriately to early-warning signs of conflict, since they have the potential to inflame, reduce motivation and cause inefficiency.

Assertive behaviour is the one most likely to lead to a result that will be acceptable to all because it is based on going for a win-win and is often the optimal approach. The term 'assertive' is commonly used derogatively. However, assertiveness is aimed at respecting the views and needs of other people as well as expressing and clarifying your own needs; it is not just about standing up for yourself. Expressing what you want plainly to clarify needs is a good thing for another person to hear. Ideally, assertive behaviour alone would meet all circumstances.

Where people have different views or needs, matched with the responsive behaviours discussed in Chapter 2 (influencing skills), assertiveness is the most effective and successful set of behaviours for the long term. By dealing with people on the basis of mutual respect, you access a powerful way to get the outcome you need for those issues that really matter to you. Adopting an aggressive approach will result only in reciprocal aggression without a set of responsive behaviours to counterbalance it. Charming someone into collaborating may be more rewarding.

If you are going to tackle someone assertively, what you say and do will have considerable effect; you need to plan assertion carefully to avoid or overcome conflict:

- Try very hard to leave emotion out of the process and stick to businesslike language.
- Avoid generalizations and exaggeration.
- Avoid being overly critical – we all make mistakes that we learn from.

It's important to focus on the issue and not the person; you are paid by your organization to produce business benefits, but not paid to like everyone.

Let's look at the construction and behaviours typical of an **assertive approach** in more detail:

- **Listen actively**, quiet your own ego, and make notes if necessary.
- **Demonstrate** that you are actively listening by leaning towards the other person, nodding appropriately and say appropriate things.
- Make **eye-to-eye contact** but do not stare. Maintain well-balanced eye contact and express an interest in the discussion. Typically, this is done by the use of interjections ('I see', 'indeed', 'mmm', 'ah', 'yes') or facial expression (smiles, head nods, eyebrow movements) or small gestures indicating the absorption of what is being said by others.
- Describe the circumstances of the issue in an **unemotional** and **non-judgemental** manner.
- Demonstrate that you understand the other person by **repeating some of their key words** back to them to show that you have been taking in what they are saying.

- Say what you **think** and how you **feel**. Remember that 'I think that...' is followed by a thought; but 'I feel [angry/sad/disappointed]' is describing an emotion.

- **Describe the outcome** you would like to achieve. Explain specifically what you originally wanted to happen, demonstrating how you are collaborating in resolving the issue and how the solution meets the other person's needs in your view. Check this is accurate.

- Explain the **benefits** and **consequences** of any joint solutions for each of you and for others. Describe the benefits that the organization would achieve.

- Get **sustainable agreement**. Check this is true in the view of the other party; ask whether they are left with reservations.

- **Achieve a joint diagnosis** and mobilize an agreed solution.

COACH'S TIP

Language is important...

Use 'I' rather than 'you'. Predominantly using 'you' can imply criticism and appear judgemental, so it's best used sparingly. Using 'I' puts your case for how the issue affects you, which can be powerful and less aggressive. It can also be enlightening to 'stand in the other person's shoes' and to try to see the issue from their perspective.

Types of non-assertive behaviour which a PM may observe and need to intervene on are:

- **Passive** Passive behaviour is non-assertive conduct that means not expressing our needs or opinions except in a cautious or timid way. The disadvantage of passive behaviour is that our own views are ignored and our wishes unknown or neglected. Passive people frustrate others by never letting their needs and wants be communicated, so that incorrect assumptions are made to fill the vacuum and misunderstandings occur. By not standing up for ourselves, or giving way to other people, the intent is to evade culpability for any decisions and to be disarming in the face of aggressive or indirectly aggressive behaviour by another person. As a result, we may become resentful, lose confidence in ourselves, or feel our efforts are not properly appreciated. This can lead to indirectly aggressive behaviour from a previously passive person – alternatively called 'passive-aggressive' (see below).

- **Aggressive** Aggressive behaviour is at the other end of the scale from submissive behaviour. We go in absolutely determined to make our views heard and to get our own needs met. If our approach inhibits other people from expressing their views, or meeting their needs, so be it: it is up to them to fight their own corner. The disadvantage of this type of behaviour is that any gains we make are likely to be short-term ones – even if we get what we want on this occasion. Our demonstrated lack of concern for the views and feelings of others will cause resentment. That resentment will, in turn, result in a lack of co-operation or a determination to make life difficult for us in future. Aggressive behaviour must be nipped in the bud. Bullying (harassment at work) is illegal in the UK and in many other countries.

- **Passive-aggressive** This indirectly aggressive behaviour may be hard to spot in its mildest forms. It can be as subtle as non-verbal communication, gestures, eye movements, huffing or facial gestures. It can be as unsubtle as 'the smiling axe murderer' expression, sarcasm, making hostile or humiliating jokes and other indirect expressions of hostility. It may be deployed because of long-term passive behaviour creating a pressure-cooker effect in a submissive individual. Eventually, the resentment at being bullied or ignored gets too much and the desire for payback emerges in the form of indirectly aggressive behaviours.

As a PM, you should be aware of staff interactions between team members of this type and investigate its root cause for urgent remedial intervention. Given the benefits of productive behaviour (explained in Chapter 2 at some length), why do people choose types of behaviour other than assertive and responsive behaviours?

Here are some typical reasons for **passive behaviour**:

The individual...

- wants to be liked
- wants to avoid upsetting someone else
- has a fear of unpleasantness, conflict or confrontation
- has a fear of being wrong, and of the consequences
- has a fear of being in the spotlight
- assumes that another person is always right
- has never yet won an argument with another person
- doesn't want to seem aggressive or domineering
- doesn't know how to be assertive or not be submissive.

COACH'S TIP

Weighing the risks

Sometimes, it may be best to adopt a submissive role; by refusing open confrontation, you may gain the chance to choose a better time, audience or venue for a more equitable discussion.

COACHING SESSION 28

Reflection: passive behaviour

Use the space provided to add your thoughts on passive behaviour. Have you had to be passive in a relationship or situation? Have you observed it in others? Note any other reasons that you recall or have observed team members or other interested parties using to justify the behaviour.

_____

_____

_____

_____

_____

_____

_____

_____

_____

_____

_____

Here are some typical reasons for **aggressive behaviour**:

The individual...

- has a fear of being seen as weak
- likes to be feared and gets a visceral high
- use it as a strategy because it has worked in the past
- has a hidden emotional upset, stress or frustration
- enjoys a good fight, and likes winning and others losing

- likes being the centre of attention

- responds to someone appearing as prey (because they are submissive and are not taking responsibility)

- has a fear of being proved wrong or thwarted

- doesn't know how to be assertive or not be aggressive

- doesn't know how not to be aggressive without fear of being seen as submissive.

COACHING SESSION 29

Reflection: aggressive behaviour

Use the space provided to add your thoughts on aggressive behaviour. Have you become aggressive in a relationship or a situation? What are the triggers to that behaviour – a person, a place, a sensitive word? Note anything surfacing from within: your inner doubting voice and fears. Note any other reasons that you recall or have observed others saying. Have you observed aggression between team members or other interested parties in the project?

_____

_____

_____

_____

_____

_____

_____

_____

_____

_____

There may be occasions when accommodating someone else's needs at the expense of your own is the most apt outcome at that time. However, this can be stressful to endure if your own needs go unrecognized or unmet. While it can be argued that no single type of behaviour suits all circumstances, be prepared to choose the right behaviour for the particular circumstances. Usually, this will be an appropriately assertive and responsive set of behaviours. Conflict resolution strategies are not complicated to put into practice – several strategies follow in the rest of this chapter.

PREDICTING CONFLICT IN TRANSFORMATIONAL FLOW

The opportunities for conflict to arise can be inferred from the transformational flowchart shown in Figure 4.1. You can imagine the kinds of conversations that would need to take place in your organization to successfully deliver all of the project work to the business.

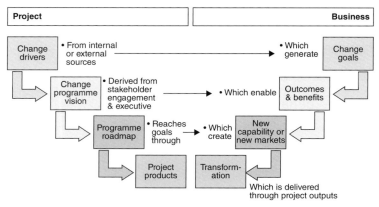

Figure 4.1 Transformational flow

Prevention is a good investment of time. Prevention, rather than cure, demonstrates foresight of the potential conflict that could arise in workplace situations. Most reasonably experienced people can look at the agenda to a meeting, workshop or seminar and know which topics will be contentious.

Conflict typically takes the following forms:

■ **Intrapersonal conflict** This type of conflict affects the individual alone. For example, a situation may arise that has two equally attractive alternatives. On the other hand, it may be that the alternatives are equally poor!

■ **Interpersonal conflict** This occurs between one or more individuals, and is a major form of conflict faced by most managers given the highly interpersonal nature of their job.

■ **Inter-group conflict** This can occur between different groups or parts of an organization. It may be that the groups have different goals, or different method of working and so on.

- **Inter-organizational conflict** One obvious example is competition for business. Another may be between employer and unions, or government regulatory authorities, industry and commerce.

In relation to the change programme, think about the personalities and any politics, posturing or careful positioning going on in your organization right now.

COACHING SESSION 30

Potential points of conflict

Looking at the transformational flow where different project products are related to business changes, use the space provided to note which you consider to be potential points of conflict or confrontation:

_____

_____

_____

_____

_____

_____

_____

_____

_____

_____

_____

_____

_____

_____

_____

_____

_____

_____

_____

_____

COACHING SESSION 31

Predicting points of conflict

Use the following table to pinpoint and cross-reference potential types of conflict which may arise with transformation tasks and products or adapt the template downloadable from www.consultationltd.com/PMCoach to record your thoughts on stakeholders or team members and decide your courses of action.

Type of conflict → / Transformational flow assigned task ↓	Intrapersonal	Interpersonal	Inter-group	Inter-organizational
Change drivers				
Change goals				
Change programme vision				
Outcomes and benefits				

Type of conflict → / Transformational flow assigned task ↓	Intrapersonal	Interpersonal	Inter-group	Inter-organizational
Programme roadmap or definition				
New capability				
New markets				
Project products				
Transformation (e.g. future state, target operating model)				

WHAT IS A RESPONSIBILITY ASSIGNMENT MATRIX?

A Responsibility Assignment Matrix (RAM) is used:

■ to delegate tasks, activities, products, milestones or decisions to project team members

■ to identify who makes decisions and communicate it to all stakeholders so that there is no doubt about where authority resides

■ to assign support roles

■ to clarify expectations regarding project team members' level of participation, their need to be communicated with and their accountability for decisions or delivery

■ to proactively reduce the likelihood of conflict arising in the team and the organization by making clear who does what, why and when.

Because it is a significant contributor to a conflict-free environment for a project, it is strongly recommended that a RAM is created as a part of the set-up stage of a project. Creating a RAM is proactive; it is a way of analysing and predicting how to get the team to work most effectively. One type of RAM is the RASCI (Responsible, Accountable, Supporting, Consulted, Informed) hierarchy. Each resource is designated a role per assigned activity.

A RAM is a document that should be shared, debated and formally agreed. It will be subject to change and must be kept up to date. Each stage should have a RASCI chart for the work packages and activities for that stage (see Figure 4.2). It can be costed since the cost of producing a product also includes a cost for agreeing it, quality-assuring it and other activities such as those in the communication plan.

Let's take a look at how roles are broken down using RASCI:

Ⓡ Responsible participants are assigned the task or activity.

Responsible members are persons whose contributions and efforts result in a tangible deliverable or completed task. They are allocated as the 'build' resource in the project plan because they have a broad knowledge base of the task at hand. For each task or activity, only one team member should be assigned the responsible role. A less experienced individual could be assigned to support them as part of their mentoring and development.

Ⓐ Accountable members are the people who make the final decisions and have ultimate ownership of the project.

They may be referred to as 'Approvers' or 'Approving Authorities'. They are people who make the final decision and have ultimate ownership of the project. They are individuals whose approval of the work is required *before* the task or activity is considered completed. Accountable members are the people in the spotlight – the first ones called upon if something goes wrong and the first ones showered with praise for the successes.

Ⓢ **Support participants are assigned to provide services to the PM and the project team in administering the project, the management information, co-ordinating the logistics and the quality or cost-accounting for project products.**

They are people such as the project or programme administration and support staff or other business-as-usual co-ordinators who benefit the project by being kept in the loop and who may offer services to the PM that co-ordinate with the business operation outside of the change management function.

Ⓒ **Consulted members are persons who must be consulted before a decision is finalized and action taken.**

They can provide counsel to the PM and project team, and their contributions are in the form of specialist knowledge or expertise. There can be more than one, and their input is essential to moving the task forward to successful completion.

Ⓘ **Informed members are informed that a decision or an action has been taken.**

These are information-only participants or recipients of one-way communication. These people need to be kept updated even though they have no direct or indirect role in the activity. These people need to be notified of important decisions and to receive regular status reports, even though they are informed only after a decision has been made. They do not need to be formally consulted, do not contribute directly to the decision, and do not support the task completion.

Role →/Assigned task ↓	Project manager	Sponsor	Team member	Key stakeholder	Programme office	Project support	CIO
Develop and agree business case	R	A	S	C	S/C	S	C
Develop and agree project plan	R	A	S	C	C	S	C
Develop and agree communications plan	R	A	S	C	S	C	I

Role →/Assigned task ↓	Project manager	Sponsor	Team member	Key stakeholder	Programme office	Project support	CIO
Define business requirements	C	A	R	A	S	S	C

Figure 4.2 Sample RASCI chart

THE EMOTIONAL ROOTS OF CONFLICT

Unless we delve into the emotional roots of our behaviour, we are doomed to misunderstand why we do things. We need the foresight to identify situations that may have pitfalls for us and develop specific strategies that allow us to rehearse our responses. Consider how awkward it feels to have to act constantly with hindsight – to reflect on your recent conduct and to repair relationships or even contractual agreements? Unless you get to these emotional roots, you are doomed to be looking backwards and trying to patch things up for life. Choose how you want to be – proactively.

The following sections and exercises may feel like child's play but they are, in my experience, enormously powerful in enabling people to express themselves assertively. They allow you to investigate and become more knowledgeable about people and about how the potential for upsets can be reduced or even eliminated. They ask the questions: 'How do emotions affect us?' and 'Why are upsets sustained and not resolved?'

Identify the emotional needs underlying an upset by:

- understanding the causes of upsets and the emotional needs
- understanding payoffs – the reasons why upsets are sustained.

Look at the following table:

Cause of upsets	Emotional needs
Miscommunication	To be heard and understood
Thwarted ambition	To achieve things
Unmet emotional needs	To be supported by people
Incomplete information	To be told what you need to know
Undelivered communication	For the other person to hear what *you* need and want

ΩΩ COACHING SESSION 32

Self-assessment: causes of upsets and the needs behind them

Complete the following table by matching five upsets that you have had in the last year to the causes listed in the table above, or add another cause, as you see fit.

Example cause of upsets	Your emotional needs at the time
1. Miscommunication	
2. Thwarted ambition	
3. Unmet emotional needs	
4. Incomplete information	
5. Undelivered communication	

⊖⊖ COACHING SESSION 33

Self-assessment: an example of conflict

As the PM, your ability to stay calm, remain focused and be emotionally grounded in the face of disagreement or conflict is essential but not always easy. Can you maintain balance even in the midst of disagreement?

Think of a situation of conflict in your organization.

1. What happened?

_____

_____

_____

_____

_____

2. Were you the difficult person?

_____

_____

_____

_____

_____

3. How do you respond to antagonism if others tried to provoke you or other people?

_____

_____

_____

_____

4. How did the meeting chairperson handle it (if that role was not held by you)?

_____

_____

_____

_____

_____

5. What does it feel like to stay in control when there is conflict around you?

_____

_____

_____

_____

_____

6. If you did not manage self-control, did you catch yourself in the act or do you agree you are in a reflection-and-repair situation?

_____

_____

_____

_____

_____

7. If you did not achieve an ideal outcome, what can be salvaged from what occurred?

_____

_____

_____

_____

_____

8. What have you learned from this upset and how it was handled?

_____

_____

_____

_____

_____

COACHING SESSION 34

Self-assessment: causes of upset and emotional needs

Look back at the transformational flow where you identified types of conflict related to a project product or business outcome. Use the space provided here to match causes of upset and unmet emotional needs that you identify or infer are present in relationships with stakeholders or other parties.

_____

_____

_____

_____

_____

_____

_____

_____

Identify what actions you plan to take to remedy the relationship issues.

_____

_____

_____

_____

_____

_____

_____

_____

_____

_____

_____

Understanding payoffs

A payoff is a rewarding gut feeling or subconscious impetus that leads a person to sustain an upset between people. Payoffs that sustain upsets are:

Payoff more passive than aggressive	Payoff more aggressive than passive
Getting to be right	Getting to make someone else wrong
Getting to play the victim or martyr	Getting to victimize someone
Stonewalling – avoiding sharing feelings	Getting to leave someone confused or frustrated
Getting revenge for a thwarted ambition	Getting to dominate someone else

Ask yourself: can upsets be resolved productively without being honest about your feelings and motives?

PROACTIVE CLARIFICATION OF NEED

Use this time-saving table to clarify someone's intention when they have come to your desk or approached you elsewhere.

When you come to me ...

Is this for my information only?	Is this for my action – review, input, etc.?	Do you want a solution?
Do you want me to help you find a solution?	Do you want a sounding board?	Do you just want to vent your feelings?
Do you want me to talk this over with you?	Do you want me to coach or train you to do it yourself?	Do you want me to go into bat and advocate for you with someone else?

(*Source:* Navigate NZ)

GOOD WORKING RELATIONSHIPS

Teamwork is about achieving common goals and there are signs to watch for if this is not occurring; it's important that goals are:

- clear to all (unambiguous)
- understood by all
- communicated to all
- jointly owned by all
- consistent with and for everyone in the team.

COACHING SESSION 35

Team exercise: ownership of team goals

Explore with your team the amount of ownership of team goals. (There are common pitfalls such as unassigned, disparate or incompatible tasks, mismatched expectations, and inequitable and conflicting goals.) Take note of the results and your intended actions in the spaces provided.

1. The extent to which goals are defined, quantified and deliverable.

_____

_____

_____

_____

_____

_____

_____

2. The extent to which goals are shared, unambiguous or consistent.

_____

_____

_____

_____

_____

3. The extent of goal conflict or divergence.

_____

_____

_____

_____

_____

COACHING SESSION 36

Team exercise: understanding team roles

1. Do all members understand what they and others are to do to accomplish the task? (A Responsibility Assignment Matrix (RASCI) chart is essential here, whether it is a normal operation or a project.)

2. Do they know their individual responsibilities and limits of authority? (Terms of reference which include delegated limits of authority and liaison relationships as well as functional reporting lines really help.)

In new teams, time should be spent discussing and defining roles and responsibilities; this is particularly important in projects where there are milestones and delivery dates looming. As the team develops, it is typical for individuals to build expectations and assumptions of others which are seldom recorded anywhere; tasks assigned at group level do not get done – there needs to be a name in the frame.

COACH'S TIP

Tell-tale signs

In teams where responsibilities are poorly defined, there is a power vacuum – members act independently and avoid responsibility. The reporting structure will begin to see duplication as reports are filed month on month, or, equally, gaps may emerge near delivery dates.

Once team members know what they are to do and who is to do it, they must determine how they will work together. The RASCI chart helps with the workflow as well as delineating responsibility levels. Typical considerations are:

- **Decision-making** How will each of the team members participate in decision–making?

- **Communication** What messages should be communicated within the team, to whom, by what method, how much, when and how frequently?

- **Meetings** What is the team trying to achieve (customer delivery, internal milestone)? What are the agenda items to be covered? Who is responsible for each item? Was there preparatory work and how will the meeting be conducted? Who should attend?

- **Management style** The leader and the team agree the most appropriate style to meet the situation and the leader should be open to receiving feedback from the team.

In teams where workflow management is poor, meetings are unproductive or poorly attended, decision-making is dominated by one or two people, actions are taken without planning, communication is one-way, while actions are not summarized at the end of discussions so there is no productive outcome.

The quality of interaction among team members is patchy, too. As team members work together, relationships often become strained. Individual members must have ways of resolving issues to ensure that good working relationships continue.

Sometimes relationship problems occur because of a difference in values or a personality or management style clash. Managers may need to take an active role in soothing relationships during times of conflict. The more energy that is siphoned off because of bad feelings, attitudes or strong emotions, the less energy is available for the team's task.

USING BELBIN TEAM INVENTORIES IN RESOURCE ALLOCATION

Team development is a process aimed at improving team performance – your role as a PM is to identify where your focus for team development needs to be. The PM has to assign staff to project tasks, monitor their performance and release staff from a project as needed. The nature of work changes from one stage to the next in the project lifecycle, as different technical specialists' skills are required and then rolled off the project.

Conflict may occur because of differing expectations among team members. For this reason, responsibilities and boundaries should be discussed, agreed upon and promulgated. Overlapping roles can create conflict, especially when two or more team members see themselves as the expert on site and responsible for the same tasks; boundaries must be established in scope, context, timeframe or other delineation. Modern technology makes it easy to inform team members of new joiners and responsibility changes.

People contribute best in the team roles that suit them the most, not solely in terms of their technical skills but also in terms of how they prefer to behave, contribute and interrelate with others. An tool such as that developed by the British management theorist Meredith Belbin can be utilized during different project stages to assess team roles. Ideally, the PM should take the time needed to undertake such assessments, to avoid clashes of personality or frustrating people by misunderstanding them.

A summary of the Belbin Team Role descriptions can be found in Figure 4.3 below:

Team Role		Contribution	Allowable Weaknesses
Plant		Creative, imaginative, free-thinking. Generates ideas and solve difficult problems.	Ignores incidentals. Too preoccupied to communicate effectively.
Resource Investigator		Outgoing, enthusiastic, communicative. Explores opportunities and develops contacts.	Over-optimistic. Loses interest once initial enthusiasm has passed.
Co-ordinator		Mature, confident, identifies talent. Clarifies goals. Delegates effectively.	Can be seen as manipulative. Offloads own share of the work.
Shaper		Challenging, dynamic, thrives on pressure. Has the drive and courage to overcome obstacles.	Prone to provocations. Offends people's feelings.
Monitor Evaluator		Sober, strategic and discerning. Sees all options and judges accurately.	Lacks drive and ability to inspire others. Can be overly critical.
Teamworker		Co-operative, perceptive and diplomatic. Listens and averts friction.	Indecisive in crunch situations. Avoids confrontation.
Implementer		Practical, reliable, efficient. Turns ideas into actions and organises work that needs to be done.	Somewhat inflexible. Slow to respond to new possibilities.
Completer Finisher		Painstaking, conscientious, anxious. Searches out errors. Polishes and perfects.	Inclined to worry unduly. Reluctant to delegate.
Specialist		Single-minded, self-starting, dedicated. Provides knowledge and skills in rare supply.	Contributes only on a narrow front. Dwells on technicalities.

Figure 4.3 Belbin Team Role summary descriptions (© Belbin Associates 2011 (www.belbin.com))

The Belbin Team Inventory can be used online for the whole team, but a little thinking can be applied in advance of this by relating your reaction to a team role description with the nature of the work in your project stages.

COACHING SESSION 37

The Belbin Team Roles and project stages

Once you have absorbed the Belbin Team Roles, try completing the following table. If you know your team or they know one other, this can be an invaluable exercise. I have given an example.

Belbin Team Role(s)	Project stage/activity
Completer Finisher	Test strategy, test plan, test scripts, test data, user acceptance stage, test results (review of). Quality strategy, quality plan, quality control, quality assurance, quality criteria, product descriptions, peer review. Project financial accounting, costs versus benefits, business case drafting, benefit attainment tracking and investment appraisal.

STAGES OF TEAM FORMATION

Developed by Bruce Wayne Tuckman, 'Tuckman's Stages' is a long-established and widely accepted theory of team formation. It can be vital tool for the PM who seeks to proactively resolve conflict. The early stages described below can be moved through very quickly by a skilled people manager in order that the team norms and starts performing as soon as possible.

1. **Forming** A set of people come together for a specific purpose. Alternatively, one or more new members join an existing team, which has to form again as a result.

2. **Storming** Individuals discover the diversity among their colleagues and may not be equipped to deal with it or understand how to use differences beneficially. As a result, confrontations can occur, along with controversy, frustration, miscommunication and disagreement.

3. **Norming** The utility of differences emerge and individuals are utilized appropriately, achieving results. The team has formed and normed successfully.

4. **Performing** The team gets a buzz about them and they know how to tackle work together using different strengths, know-how, talents and knowledge.

5. **Adjourning/Mourning** Tuckman added this stage some years after he first proposed the original theory. A successfully formed team means that grieving takes place once it is disbanded. If team members miss each other, then you know that you got it right when you built a team in the first place.

It is very important to realize that the leadership style must adapt to the changing situation, too; the authority of the leader diminishes over the stages while the freedom and empowerment of the team members increases. Thus, in the first stage, Forming, your leadership style would need to be inspiring and visionary as you direct the newly formed team members as they establish their roles and interrelationships, and as you settle each of them into their role. Then, as the team matures and the capability begins to normalize into everyday routines, the PM can become more participative and collaborative rather than directive – delegating as much as possible and divesting tasks to team leaders.

The most common complaints associated with ineffective teamwork are the following:

■ Social loafing such as lack of motivation, co-operation, negotiation, contribution and dependence on others where team members are not doing their share of the work and thus not contributing fairly.

■ Team members acting as 'passengers' who behave parasitically towards other team members even though they may have equivalent cognitive ability and experience.

There are four types of 'debilitating effects' on teamwork in ineffective teams, though team members may often be unaware of what is happening.

The **Free Rider Effect** is where one team member is particularly talented and initially hardworking. However, other team members are less talented, and the less able members feel that their efforts are dispensable in comparison. What happens is that they expend decreasing amounts of effort, relying on the talented, motivated member to complete the task instead. The conscientious member reduces their cognitive efforts because they know that the team's product will be anchored by the inability of the less able team members. Essentially, the team produces a lesser product as a result and never performs well as a team.

The **Sucker Effect** debilitates the performance of a particular team member when a more able, hardworking team member discovers that they are being left to do all the work for the whole team. They gradually expend less effort to avoid being taken advantage of because they resent being exploited by other team members who may be equally intelligent and able. The Sucker Effect occurs either when the more able member believes that the others are capable but do not try very hard, or when they believe that the others show poor performance because of poorer ability than their own. Essentially, the team produces a lesser product and never really performs well as a team.

The **Status Differential Effect** debilitates the performance of the whole team. The Status Differential effect occurs in mixed-ability teams working on additive tasks. The perceived high ability of certain members creates status sensitivities. The higher-status members dominate the team's processes and become communication centres because they give and receive more help than the lower-status members. Consequently, the high-status members gain additional social influence and this is manifested in their impact on the team's product. The low-status members interact less and influence group processes and products less. This effect has been said to show that in teamwork the 'rich get richer and the poor get poorer'.

The **Ganging-up Effect** debilitates the performance of the whole team; it occurs when only one member likes or values the task. The intra-team conflict is resolved by the other team members subscribing to a least-effort solution, finding ways to go through the motions with the minimum cognitive expenditure. The team agrees (albeit subconsciously) that, if one member wants to do the task or obtain the reward, they complete the work. But if that team member also wants co-operation, they have to tolerate and accommodate the other members' poor interest in the task and associated reward. Paradoxically, the non-supporters expend considerable effort in negotiating a least-effort contribution in order to successfully avoid the effort they were expected to expend in pursuit of the task and associated reward. Bizarre behaviour, to say the least, but more common than you might think.

♀♀ COACHING SESSION 38

Self-assessment: team formation

A PM needs to get their team performing as quickly as possible because of the time pressures in a project. Identify any development needs so that you start demonstrating greater ability to create a well-performing team as early as possible after resource changes and team start-ups.

1. Identify your past performance in either forming a team or being part of a new team formation.

   _____

   _____

   _____

   _____

   _____

2. Identify the things that you need to do more often or do less of to be more successful at running a team.

   _____

   _____

   _____

   _____

   _____

3. Identify the consequences of failing to form a team well, either from past experience or from your thinking having read this chapter.

   _____

   _____

   _____

   _____

DIMENSIONS OF CO-OPERATION AND ASSERTIVENESS

In conflict situations, we can describe a person's behaviour along two basic dimensions:

- **Assertive behaviour** – the extent to which the individual attempts to satisfy his or her own concerns

- **Co-operative behaviour** – the extent to which the individual attempts to satisfy the other person's concerns; a co-operative response recognizes the needs of an individual or a group.

The co-operative dimension could be said to reflect the importance of the *relationship* while the assertive dimension might reflect the importance of an *issue*.

These two dimensions of behaviour can be used to define five methods of dealing with conflict. Figure 4.4 illustrates the five possible approaches to conflict, reflecting different degrees of willingness to be assertive and/or co-operative.

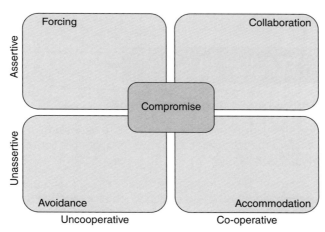

Figure 4.4 Dimensions of co-operation and assertiveness (*source:* Blake and Moulton (1964))

- **Forcing** is both assertive and uncooperative. It can be described as working against the wishes of another party. It is focused on satisfying one's own needs, fighting to dominate in a win-lose competition, or forcing things to a favourable conclusion through the exercise of one's authority.

- **Collaboration** is both assertive and co-operative. This is the attempt to fully satisfy the concerns of all parties. This is often referred to as 'problem-solving' mode. The aim is to find the underlying causes of the conflict and resolve them, rather than to find fault or apportion blame. In this way, both sides can feel that they have 'won'.

- **Compromise** is neither assertive nor unassertive, nor is it co-operative or uncooperative. Compromise works towards partial satisfaction of everyone's concerns; seeking 'acceptable' rather than 'optimal' solutions so that no one totally wins or completely loses. This tends to produce expedient rather than effective solutions and leaves people feeling disquieted more than satisfied.

- **Avoidance** is both unassertive and uncooperative. This stance neglects the interests of all parties by side-stepping conflict and postpones any chance of conflict resolution; it solves nothing. This may happen if you refuse to participate in the situation or you attempt to stay neutral at all costs.

- **Accommodation** is unassertive and co-operative. By letting the other party's wishes rule, you neglect your own requirements. This may involve appeasement, conciliation or mollification by attempting to smooth over differences and thus maintain a superficial harmony. In the short term, there is a cessation of hostilities but the other party has had their sense of power reinforced by your behaviour – by not asserting your own needs, they remain unconsidered. In the long term, accommodating behaviour can be damaging and unsatisfying and lead to bottled-up frustration.

COACHING SESSION 39

Dimensions of co-operation and assertiveness

From your experience of organizational life, try to think of one example of conflict where the response fitted each of the following categories: forcing, collaboration, compromise, avoidance, accommodation.

Briefly describe the nature of the conflict in the space provided and also the effect of adopting the style used. In addition, comment on whether a different style would have resulted in a 'better' resolution of the conflict.

1. **Forcing** (assertive, uncooperative)

_____

_____

_____

_____

_____

_____

_____

_____

2. **Collaboration** (assertive, co-operative)

_____

_____

_____

_____

_____

_____

3. **Compromise** (neither assertive/unassertive nor co-operative/uncooperative)

_____

_____

_____

_____

_____

_____

4. **Avoidance** (unassertive, uncooperative)

_____

_____

_____

_____

_____

_____

5. **Accommodation** (unassertive, co-operative)

_____

_____

_____

_____

_____

_____

Now identify any development needs, so that you start demonstrating greater ability to work with others:

6. Identify the things that you do that breach trust or break teamwork and collaboration with employees and other colleagues.

_____

_____

_____

_____

_____

_____

7. Identify the things that you need to do to be more collaborative or what behaviour needs to be curbed.

_____

_____

_____

_____

_____

_____

8. Identify what is the cost of being under strength at teamwork and the consequences for the team.

_____

_____

_____

_____

_____

_____

NEXT STEPS

The first three chapters suggested that motivating staff and influencing stakeholders effectively are proactive ways of getting work done well and of reducing the chances of conflict arising or having an unfortunate outcome. This chapter addressed the circumstance where PMs arrive on projects after they have started and are given a team of people as a fait accompli. While PMs may not be able to choose their own team, they can learn to understand personality traits, work with them and motivate individuals to maximize the whole team's performance.

This chapter's content addressed the PM as a leader of people, offering tools to reduce the likelihood of confrontations arising and sufficient know-how to resolve disputes intelligently.

The following chapter addresses the project definition and communication planning requirements and the documents, workshops, wall charts or other useful artefacts that help people grasp what the project is about.

👍 TAKEAWAYS

How do you rate your conflict handling style in terms of dimensions in co-operation and assertiveness?

_____

_____

_____

_____

_____

_____

_____

_____

_____

_____

_____

Are you able to match your behaviour to the circumstance? Which skills do you need to improve, if any?

_____

_____

_____

_____

_____

_____

_____

_____

_____

_____

_____

_____

Identify specifically what points of conflict can you predict from the transformational flow model (Figure 4.1) or your own modified version of it – what changes need to be made to avoid or resolve conflict?

_____

_____

_____

_____

_____

_____

_____

_____

_____

_____

Which tool will be the greatest asset to the project in terms of preventing conflict and why – a Responsibility Assignment Matrix, Belbin or team formation stages, or another?

_____

_____

_____

_____

_____

_____

_____

_____

_____

_____

_____

_____

_____

_____

END-TO-END COMMUNICATIONS PLANNING

5

 OUTCOMES FROM THIS CHAPTER

- Identify the best business outcome and change drivers for your project.

- Identify the relationship between communications planning, a project's lifecycle and the project products' lifespan and its replacement.

- Understand why an end-to-end communications strategy extends beyond a project's lifecycle and is thereby seamless.

- Complete an exercise to establish a clear purpose for your project.

- Develop an initial communications plan using a template.

- Appreciate that the communication plan can be further developed as the project progresses into an integrated communications strategy and into multiple campaign plans.

A communication strategy is a vital aspect without which PMs are unlikely to succeed. Communicating insufficiently or ineffectively is one of the most common reasons why business transformations fail. Even while the majority of cost is expended in the project phases followed by benefit phases when the product is available for in-service use, the communications plan must be seamless and fully funded (or tightly estimated). You will have to research your own organization using the principles set out in this chapter as there will be a large variety of differences between one organization and market and another. Use of the term 'end-to-end communications' in this workbook covers both the project's lifecycle plus the product's lifespan (i.e. the outputs, outcomes or deliverables).

WHAT TYPE OF CHANGE PROJECT DOES YOUR ORGANIZATION NEED?

If you fail to communicate the purpose of the change with clarity (despite your carefully created vision), employees will not act in line with your hopes and expectations. The communication deficiencies can be about the frequency of messages, the targeting of a message to a particular stakeholder's agenda, the choice of channel aimed at a group's demographics, or a lack of integration across channels.

The best business outcome

In order to succeed, the PM needs to focus on those items that may deliver the best business outcome with the most feasible and auditable benefits.

- An outcome is the state of the organization or a community as a result of change that is different to the previous state.

- An outcome can be observable behavioural changes or a change in the circumstances of the organization (market share, new enablers, relocation, repurposing, legal status, operating basis, structure, partnering or supply chain change).

COACHING SESSION 40

The business outcome for your project

Describe the business outcome for your project in a nutshell, much as you would explain it in the opening minutes of a meeting with a stakeholder.

_____

_____

_____

_____

Let's face it, people quite naturally resist change; the more comfortable they are with the status quo, the more they will disbelieve the need to make any changes. So it is essential that you communicate throughout a change programme and before major events. Failing to communicate efficiently and effectively is one of the most common reasons why business transformations fail.

Change drivers

Unless you are already crystal clear on your change drivers, you need to establish an agreed purpose and to develop a two-way communications plan for your project. There are many distinct reasons why organizations have to transform themselves or have to make significant changes by using a temporary structure and change team. The reasons are part of a joint diagnosis of change drivers and the selection of an appropriate methodology or lifecycle for mobilization. This chapter provides a series of coaching sessions that allow you to think these matters through and to draft documentation.

COACHING SESSION 41

Diagnose the change drivers for your project

Tick which of the following examples apply to your project and add your own reasons in the space provided.

1. To respond to external changes (e.g. political, economic, societal, technology, legal, environmental, market forces)

2. To alter the organization's structure or ways of working in partnership

3. To engender attitudinal changes

4. To effect changes in understanding of the way things are done (policies, workflow, process, procedures, funding basis)

5. To engender behavioural changes to become or to match a new culture (such as in an acquisition or merger scenario) ☐

_____

_____

_____

6. Other reason

_____

_____

_____

If you've been unable to diagnose the change drivers so far, later exercises will assist you to do so.

COACHING SESSION 42

Build a picture of the purpose of your project

Answer the following questions, using each theme to build a clear picture of the purpose of your project, and what the scope is of your communications plan. If you are unable to answer the following sets of questions, then your stakeholders are unlikely to have grasped a clear sense of purpose.

Theme	Answer
THEME 1: The personal aspects of strategic change	
What does this change mean?	

Theme	Answer
What is it like for me to experience this change?	
THEME 2: The organizational context	
Where is our organization now in relation to this intended change?	
What are we trying to become?	

Theme	Answer
What are we trying to do?	
How are we going about the journey between now and where we want to be, and by when?	

Theme 2 posed organizational context questions such as 'What are we trying to become?' Theme 3 deals with follow-through questions and answers. If the answer to the above question was that organization wanted to become agile, then the next questions would be:

THEME 3: The organizational aspects of change	
What does an agile organization look like?	

Theme	Answer
How do we rate our current level of agility?	
How do we assess our current change ability or change readiness?	
Now that we have carried through assessments, what are the implications for our organization of being where we are in terms of change readiness, agility and maturity?	

Theme	Answer
THEME 4: Making the transition	
What issues do we face in making the transition?	
What obstacles lie in our path?	
How do we work together to achieve shared goals?	

Theme	Answer
What resources or tools will make collaboration more effective and efficient?	
THEME 5: Personal transition	
What is the nature of the change to me (new skills, status, role, attitude or behaviour)?	
What will the changes mean to me (sense of loss/ gain, excitement, new aspirations)?	

Theme	Answer
How congruent are the plans we are making with my personal situation?	
What are the key challenges and issues for me?	
What support will I need to make and sustain this change?	
What will my personal action plan look like?	

One of the most important things to get your head around is that you have to accept that there will be an emotional response to most business change announcements. Look at Figure 5.1.

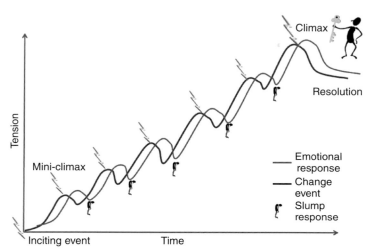

Figure 5.1 Change arc with response arc

The top line on the chart shows events as 'mini-climax' points that happen to your organization as a response to external or internal forces for change. The line underneath shows as an example 'people's slump' response to those 'mini-climax' events; the emotional response could be another strong emotion such as anger or unrest. Now this change and response arc is just one view of a project timeline (technical lifecycles are covered later); however, this is a view that is less commonly taken.

It is rather like the three-act structure of a blockbuster book, film or play, where there will be:

■ people who want to become heroes and end up being regarded as heretics

■ changes to the plot (an action sequence involving and affecting key players)

■ a resulting emotional response to the plot from the main characters (forming their emotional journey).

As a change leader, working with your sponsor in particular, you can manage these 'change and response' arcs so that you work towards a sustainable resolution. These announcements are the kinds of events that should be predicted, and countermeasures to unhelpful responses should be scheduled and funded. You will be identify these as you complete your communications plan later in this chapter.

The nature of managing users' or customers' expectations is sometimes like climbing a massive mountain peak; after scaling one hill after another, you realize that the visible horizon is the top of hill you are on at present and not the top of the mountain peak itself. Managing expectations requires:

- well-honed management skills with stakeholders including clients
- psychologically astute management of the people aspects of strategic change
- communications strategy, plans, channels, tools, resources and skills
- benefits management.

There is a need for each function's own change plan – functions such as any strategic planning unit, HR, IT, Finance, Production, Sales, Marketing and so on. You might want to begin by running some executive team-building events that generate a change management plan. The wisdom behind this is to allow participants to explore what the changes feel like and how it would impact them.

Experience has taught me that apparent 'permission to change' is usually granted after 'permission to explore what this change feels like' and that those who do not recognize this tend to get sabotaged.

The requirements are:

- to create and manage the relevant communications
- to explore, negotiate and manage the business case in the initiation stage
- to predict and agree the benefits through two-way communication
- to have the skills in your team (in addition to the influencing skills and strategies as per the previous chapters) to engage stakeholders effectively (covered in more depth later).

Many organizations are more at ease with left-brain logic than those affecting the emotional centres of the brain – that is, a management or technical lifecycle for a project such as the management phases covering initiation, study of requirements and scope, then delivery. In order to ensure the change project's success, communication needs to be as seamless as possible – from the stakeholders' involvement in the early project stages and through into the product lifespan where it is in use in the organization or with customers.

The extensive scope of the end-to-end communications strategy means that you need:

- to identify the lifecycle to be used on your project
- to identify the project's products' lifespan, if appropriate to your project
- to identify your replacement strategy for it, as shown in Figure 5.2 below, if appropriate to your project.

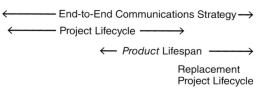

Figure 5.2 The end-to-end communications strategy

The end-to-end communications strategy encompasses:

- the project's communication plan and its implementation up to the close of the project
- the plan for the product's in-service lifespan
- the outline plan for the product's replacement project.

The communications plan is a part of the overall project plan and is just as important as the other annexes to the project plan, which are the business case, a quality plan, the risk plan and a change plan (explaining how the baseline plan can be amended and how the configuration of products is controlled). The following coaching sessions will help you:

- to identify a technical and management lifecycle
- to identify a methodology for an end-to-end communications strategy
- to create a first-draft communication plan document that suits your context, circumstances, background and environment.

It's a good idea to read through all of the coaching sessions before starting the first one, so you can see how you might be prompted and guided in your exploration and determination of what suits your circumstances.

As part of your marketing strategy, you are likely to conduct situational, market and competitor analyses for your sector, domain, customer demographics, market, industry, rivals and allies (potential or existing partners). Focus groups have been used historically to assess customer interest, but nowadays executives ask data specialists to find these insights by using new tools for analysing sales numbers, website behaviour, sensor data and social sentiment (e.g. opinions, natural language analysis and contextual polarity). This whole process has changed or is in the process of being transformed by 'big data', thereby making focus-group events a thing of the past.

A new frontier of competitive differentiation for your marketing strategy is large-scale data gathering and analytics (e.g. Google, Amazon, Netflix). By pursuing relevance and usability, we have enabled ourselves to capture the requirements of a system and make options increasingly viable in terms of the balance between business value and technical risk. Organizations and companies in a range of industries (e.g. pharmaceuticals, retail telecommunications, financial products and insurance) are progressing big-data strategies with novel strategic approaches to big data.

However, CEOs face challenges that can prevent big-data initiatives from taking root. Depending on the likely action of competitors, the high priorities in existing portfolios of projects and how this impacts strategic priorities, programmes and initiatives may predicate the need for these to be finished first.

Figure 5.3 illustrates materials that you should produce with your business or customer intelligence specialists and the communications team – events and announcements calendar/schedule, diagrammatic structures, hierarchies, dependencies and other relationships. The downloadable list of reference materials will give you additional resources describing particular methods of how to construct these types of product, if you are unfamiliar with them. Go to www.TYCoachbooks.com/ProjectManagement.

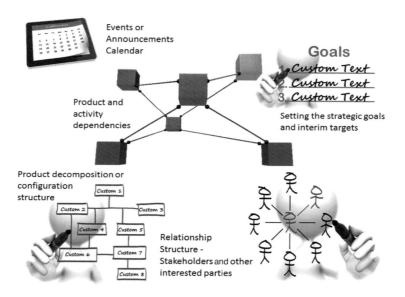

Figure 5.3 Communications materials

This planning and scheduling can only be done at high level for items further into the future; in the early stages, too much detailed work would be inconsequential for later stages. You will effectively produce a critical path or optimal sequence on a large wall chart for typically the next 18 months to two years and be able to create management milestones once you have the big picture. This can be modelled electronically if you have the computer power and right applications.

COACHING SESSION 43

Create a timeline

Create a timeline for up to two years, working with paper, flipchart or a whiteboard as this will allow you to use 'what if' scenarios to explore different options and ideas. Working backwards from the future, use sticky notes to write down desired outcomes, potential threats and opportunities (for example new competitors in your market or loss of market share owing to new technology).

If you prefer working with your hands in the early formulation of a plan, put all your ideas for activities and HR processes on to the timeline and use string, thin tape or a pen to create links. Stay high level and work out detail on separate sheets. You can take digital photographs of the timeline or get it turned into electronic form using a planning tool such as Visio.

Answer the questions on the following forms or create some of your own, making notes online or in a project workbook. By doing so, you will establish:

- a clear purpose for your project and the communication of it

- a systems development lifecycle or some other type of lifecycle appropriate to the deliverables

- documentation for your communications strategy and plan.

PROJECT LIFECYCLE

A lifecycle is a series of stages describing activities within each step. Figure 5.4 shows the four management and technical stages: initiation, study, delivery and closure.

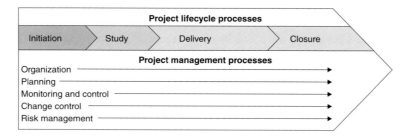

Figure 5.4 Project lifecycle processes

However, the stage names will vary according to the methodology chosen and the required product. For example, a 'design, develop or delivery' project will have resource needs such as business analysts, programmers or coders while a marketing project will have, say, market analysts, design agencies and ecommerce campaign skills.

The majority of costs occur when the products or deliverables are being constructed or procured. The tangible benefits justifying the costs as estimated are set out in the business case during project set-up or an initiation stage; this makes evident the expected timing of revenue (income) or cost avoidance (money retained and not expended).

Benefits come in during the *lifespan* of the *product* and are monitored as its performance in the market or as quality in the eyes of the internal or external customer.

The processes listed below the stage names in Figure 5.4 are explained below:

- **Organization** The structure, roles and responsibilities, relationships, delegated limits of authority.

- **Planning** All the technical lifecycle planning and scheduling requirements.

- **Monitoring and control** The daily, weekly and monthly routine monitoring and control procedures to be followed to progress through the stages after the project plan is agreed, used as a baseline for measurement of productivity and for tracking progress.

- **Change control** (including configuration management) Change, or configuration, control is the identification of configuration items and the recording of amendments to them; thus, maintaining control of version numbers during the project where one item is dependent on another. Serious operational issues will ensue if related items are not version-controlled during development or on release of program code into the live environment.

- **Risk management** Risk management consists of risk identification, analysis and evaluation, application of risk control options and risk monitoring.

- **Quality management** Last but not least is quality planning. This varies more than any other PM discipline. Each organization has its own quality path or function and this may include the International Standards Organization (ISO) model of quality management.

Your quality management function may include audit or examination of a potential supplier's quality management system prior to engaging them. There will be ad hoc audits throughout the contract, too.

You may run quality-assurance and quality-control routines throughout the development of the products such as when interim deliverables, modules and incremental developments are said to be completed.

You may use a separate supplier to run a test strategy for you to check the quality and completeness of another supplier's deliveries, treated as a separate test stage in the project.

Whatever your chosen quality policy, you must ensure that communications products go through an inspection process so that errors undermining your change objectives and corporate reputation are not adversely impacted.

These events, announcements, online media and interviews are carrying your brand into the future or stopping it short of your goals. These have to be checked without much delay as communications is a fast-moving operation, so make sure that resources are firmly allocated to do this inspection.

⚲⚲ COACHING SESSION 44

Create a diagram identifying your project's stages

Taking these planning and control considerations into account, create a diagram for your project lifecycle identifying the technical stages and listing the outputs from each stage. Use Figure 5.5 to help you, if necessary. You might like to download a project lifecycle template from www.consultationltd.com/PMCoach. If you prefer, you could use sticky notes and add them to a torn-off flipchart sheet. In this way, you can change the order, or labelling, of things at will.

If appropriate, you could show a product lifespan following on from the development project's lifecycle. If relevant, show a replacement project lifecycle as well.

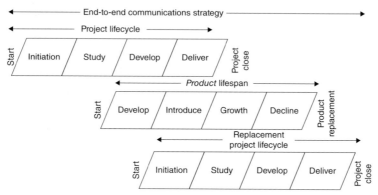

Figure 5.5 End-to-end communications strategy: project, product and replacement project lifecycles

COACH'S TIP

Running a product lifespan

If it is appropriate to run a product lifespan, involve the appropriate set of stakeholders in the preparation of the plan and the business readiness activities. Expect these people to be different from the design and development teams. You may have business readiness activities to prepare with retail outlets, customer centres, agents, brokers, an ecommerce unit and so on, as well as the service maintenance team (infrastructure). They will need training, not just notification of an upcoming product launch.

DOCUMENT DESCRIPTION OF A COMMUNICATION PLAN

In establishing a clear purpose for your project and its communications plan, you need to complete a textual narrative that clarifies your thinking and intentions so others can be briefed on the project.

In this section, you will be asked to use the answers from the previous exercises and to document them using the format below or your organization's own template.

Purpose

The result of putting a communication plan into practice is to provide the project board and PM with timely and salient management information on which to act.

The plan defines the interests of all relevant parties and describes how, when, why and how often the project team communicates with stakeholders. This includes the costs of communicating using multiple channels. Commercial communications strategies tend to be run as a series of campaigns to achieve specific purposes (such as the incremental release of new or enhanced products).

Public-sector communications tend to focus on the implementation of new political policies and initiatives and report to the wider public what progress has been made.

Regardless of whether the sector is public or private, the PM needs to be kept informed of any changes in the corporate or programme environment if these might impact the project so that appropriate action can be taken. Having two-way feedback is a massive benefit to all those responsible for running the project.

Content

The communication plan lists the details required for communication purposes of all groups with a vested interest in the project or responsible for certain aspects such as audit and quality management. Information is recorded for each identified stakeholder group or audience, including:

- the communications objective
- the group's stance, perspectives or motivations
- the messages crafted to match your communications objective
- the layout, where appropriate
- the approaches to be taken using each media and channel
- the communicators
- the timing and priority (your calendar and codification of the relative importance of events using colours or symbols)
- the feedback cycle.

Sources and quality

Until the communication needs of all stakeholders are determined, the plan is incomplete. As discussed earlier, the communication plan must align with other aspects to be planned for, such as quality, stage plans, risk planning and other aspects of complex change programmes such as cross-project dependencies. The sources for the communications plan should thus include:

- the project board members
- relevant project team members and specialist suppliers such as digital agencies
- stage plans (phases in the project plan) so that communications activities are feasibly timed in stage plans and schedules
- project management documentation specifying the permitted brief or mandate, the quality expectations, the technical approach and details of the organizational structure and environment.

THE MECHANICS OF COMMUNICATIONS

The broader project team needs skills to manage the mechanics of various channels of communication at different project stages, working with business change managers and communications professionals:

- **Press relations** Face-to-face meetings, announcements or interviews, TV, radio and press releases.
- **World Wide Web/Internet** Using your website to inform stakeholders, customers, staff and partners. A separate website is often created to manage a crisis. The core of this type of website can be designed in advance in many

cases because the likely nature of a crisis will be related to the products and services (e.g. where a supermarket product has become contaminated).

- **Social media** Many types of social media are used by employees, customers, local communities, other stakeholders or interested parties. There are plenty of case studies that show how not being proactive has put a company at a disadvantage (e.g. BP's handling of social media during the Gulf of Mexico pollution incident).

- **Shareholder events** The AGM and other meetings or large gatherings relevant to the business purpose.

- **Customer, sector and industry events** Conferences, seminars, industry bodies or user groups.

- **Stakeholder events** Focus groups, requirements gathering, design walk-throughs, 'show and tell' demonstrations (once a shippable increment or release is at a suitable stage), user training.

COACH'S TIP

Social media

Increasingly, in the age of social media you may need to recruit specialist resources to develop, implement and evaluate effective communications campaigns supporting the delivery of operational objectives.

ONLINE RESOURCE

The PM's key responsibilities – communications planning

Download a useful list of the key responsibilities of the PM concerning end-to-end communications planning.

www.TYCoachbooks.com/ProjectManagement.

COACHING SESSION 45

Design your own communications strategy

Create a communications strategy that suits your circumstances and environment, using policies and procedures at work and the following questions and guidance.

1. What type of project are you creating a communications strategy for? (See the examples at the start of this chapter.)

_____

_____

_____

_____

_____

_____

_____

2. What lifecycle stages or methodology are appropriate to produce the expected outputs, products, deliverables and/or outcomes? List them here or use an existing diagram.

_____

_____

_____

_____

_____

_____

_____

_____

3. Is it appropriate to show a product lifespan?

_____

_____

_____

_____

_____

_____

_____

_____

4. Is it your intention to use an iterative process such as agile/scrum? If so, complete the exercise in Coaching session 72 in Chapter 11.

_____

_____

_____

_____

_____

_____

_____

_____

5. Explore different options for the systems development approach.

_____

_____

_____

_____

_____

_____

6. What situation are you in?

7. Do you have interlinked programmes that need amalgamating?

8. Are programmes and projects misaligned with objectives?

9. What are the skills and experience of key personnel relevant to the content and strategic intent?

10. As the project develops, how will you acquire the skilled resources to progress this plan into an integrated communications strategy with campaign plans that craft each message to the target audience, the channel and the current project milestones?

11. Identify the relative political positions of key personnel and what impact these have (e.g. are they the optimal division or business unit for the project?).

_____

_____

_____

_____

_____

_____

If you do not communicate as frequently as stakeholders feel they need, they will make up what is happening and this can cause misunderstandings that are damaging and costly to clear up. Therefore, you need to create a calendar for the project and the in-service life of its products that identifies events or announcements and records the dates, venues and other details. You need to develop a process that highlights each event or announcement with appropriate lead time to get everything ready.

COACHING SESSION 46

Create a calendar

Create a calendar listing everything that needs to be produced for an event for each communication channel, for each group, interested parties or stakeholders. Entries might be the announcement of a merger, a new partnership or a new legal trading status for the organization; a calendar entry does not necessarily have to pertain to a physical meeting at a venue.

Use sticky notes and a flipchart or any other planning tool that suits you. The following considerations may help you during this task.

1. Identify the activities needed to produce each event product and the skills, media or tools required to complete it, and schedule them into the project plan.

_____

_____

_____

_____

_____

_____

_____

_____

_____

_____

2. Identify the dependencies between activities and the product relationships so that a critical path can be calculated for the project, product lifespan and the whole end-to-end communication strategy. Activities on the critical path have no flexibility in their completion dates without moving the project end date.

_____

_____

_____

_____

_____

_____

_____

3. Develop a process (sometimes called a 'bring-up' system) that reminds you of the event with sufficient lead time so that everything can be completed in time and to sufficient quality. This could be using a project-management tool, a spreadsheet, an office calendar/team diary manager. Make a brief note of the process here.

_____

_____

_____

_____

_____

_____

_____

The life of the product begins after the closure of the main build project (as in Figure 5.5). An output may be an interim deliverable (which needs communicating as a success), but sometimes it will be a final product to be delivered as part of satisfying the business case and the end-user or customer community.

In order to ensure the success of the products, the communications need to be as seamless as possible. So, as the programme progresses through planning phases and its implementation, you have to work with the information available to you and predict the likely emotional responses to programme, project or business events (for example, the first day a merger becomes legally enacted). Against this backdrop, the change team needs to organize the communications to all the stakeholders – principally staff but also shareholders, the wider public and media organizations.

⧉⧉ COACHING SESSION 47

Passing on the communications baton

As the product goes live, the responsibilities for coal-face communication shifts from skilled individuals in the project team to permanent PR functions in the marketing, sales or customer-service departments.

1. Who would this be in your organization and whom will they receive handovers from? You may have a business readiness spreadsheet for this or you can create one.

_____

_____

_____

_____

_____

_____

_____

_____

_____

_____

_____

2. The business benefits must still be delivered on time (a responsibility usually retained by the project's sponsor or executive). Who would this be in your organization and how will it operate?

_____

_____

_____

_____

_____

_____

_____

_____

_____

_____

_____

_____

 NEXT STEPS

In this chapter you have learned about the different types of change project and you should now understand why under-communication is one of the most common reasons that business transformations fail. You will also have developed an initial communications plan.

Chapter 6: Political intelligence complements this chapter, providing insights into mobilizing change, stakeholder management and how to engage powerfully with your sponsor using a unifying model.

TAKEAWAYS

Explain why under-communication is one of the most common reasons business transformations fail.

_____

_____

_____

_____

_____

_____

_____

_____

_____

_____

Explain what a communication plan looks like for your project.

_____

_____

_____

_____

_____

_____

_____

_____

_____

_____

Summarize the purpose for your project and what can be communicated in an integrated communications strategy and campaign plans.

_____

_____

_____

_____

_____

_____

_____

_____

_____

_____

Why should an end-to-end communications strategy extend beyond a project's lifecycle?

_____

_____

_____

_____

_____

_____

_____

_____

_____

_____

_____

_____

POLITICAL INTELLIGENCE

 OUTCOMES FROM THIS CHAPTER

- Identify the differences between line and project management.
- Identify the sources of the PM's authority.
- Clarify the type of authority required and how it will be exercised.

'Politics is not a game. It is an earnest business.'

Winston Churchill

Political intelligence is the pivotal skillset in managing stakeholders including your sponsor. Equally, deploying better political savvy can reduce stress at work for you and your team members. The day-to-day angst caused by not being as politically savvy as necessary serves as motivation enough to learn more about this sensitive subject where privacy is under your direct control. This chapter builds on preceding chapters so that you are:

- managing the motivation of your current PM team
- using your enhanced influencing skills and strategies
- combining them with smart communications planning so that you feel equipped to succeed regardless of the political landscape.

POLITICS AND PROJECT AUTHORITY FOR A CHANGE AGENT

Conceptually, the project environment is envisaged as a temporary structure where the skills required depend upon the demands of the project technical lifecycle, management stage and its duration. Sometimes the temporary nature of the structure and environments of projects, programmes or portfolios works against PMs becoming sufficiently politically aware. PMs may not have the luxury of getting to know people thoroughly in order to assess the political landscape because the validity and composition of projects, programmes or portfolios are dynamic. However, PMs need to utilize varying forms of investigation and influence to become politically aware and savvy in their actions to avoid or overcome competing resource needs and conflicting agendas.

Larger organizations may have pools of managers at different levels (project, programme and portfolio) who will be assigned based on skills, experience and availability. They will be supported by specialists with technical, financial and management skillsets related to the nature of the business (for example risk management or procurement skills). An astute PM could win over this pool of resources and support even if the people are not directly working on their project. These assets can help you to become more knowledgeable about the political agenda, likely sources of resistance and barriers, allegiances and key personnel's track records.

Working on the assumption that you would want to prevent conflict occurring, you should remember that not everyone with power has influence. What do you do with your power and authority? How do you intend to use it at the tactical level where the day-to-day application of influence is often what counts?

 COACH'S TIP

A word of caution

Your personal credibility can be easily undermined by inappropriate political behaviour.

There are a significant number of proactive things covered here which you can do. It is important to understand the different bases on which project management is measured versus line management and how this may affect your authority.

Project manager	Line manager
Task completion orientation	Resource control orientation
Lateral control, possibly with customer liaison	Vertical control, possibly with customer account control
Measured on achieving project goals within budget, time, cost and quality targets, possibly using earned value analysis in the build stage	Measured on value, availability, efficiency, effectiveness and cost of resources
Measured on ongoing productivity of stages and stakeholder engagement	Measured on ongoing turnover, profit, customer satisfaction and the absence of hassle
Bottom-line aim is 'solving the problem and delivering the goods' in a pressured timeframe	Bottom-line aim is 'caring for the value delivered by resources' or 'making the numbers in the accounts you are responsible for'

COACHING SESSION 48

Project manager versus line manager

The table above just shows examples of different perspectives and is not an 'exam answer'. How accurate a reflection is this comparison for *your* circumstances? Record your thoughts in the space provided.

_____

_____

_____

_____

_____

_____

_____

_____

_____

_____

_____

SOURCES OF PROJECT AUTHORITY

Politics are the behaviours which people use to influence others either positively or negatively. It is unwise to deny that politics exist in the workplace as this can operate against you. Become a keen observer of:

- **Good political behaviour** Become excellent at networking and stakeholder management. Build a strong and pervasive network of people who will also observe the political landscape (good and bad political behaviour).

- **Bad political behaviour** Learn to recognize people who seek advantage at other people's expense rather than acting for the greater good.

Essentially, it is recommended that you steer clear of any negative use of politics and use positive political action to promote yourself and your team. Ask yourself: 'Where do I get my power and influence from?'

Positive	Negative
Your ability to reward others	Your status or rank
Something about you which motivates people to be influenced by you	Coercion of others to do what you want
A strong and widespread network of good relationships	Your ability to punish others
Your influencing ability to persuade people to do something they would not otherwise do	Your ability to manipulate others to do something against their better judgement or free will
Your ability to share expertise with others	Your power by association with authority figures

You may also gain or be granted power and influence 'based on law' (de jure) or 'based on facts' (de facto); examples are illustrated in the table in Coaching session 49.

COACHING SESSION 49

De jure and de facto considerations

Tick which of the following are true for your organization, project and role description or terms of reference.

De jure considerations ('based on law')		De facto considerations ('based on facts')	
Organizational mission, charter or project mandate document or similar grants you rights or scope	☐	Level of technical knowledge and vital expertise	☐
Organizational position – such as being the Chief Financial Officer which may hold legal standing	☐	Rapport and engagement abilities	☐
Role description – delegated limits of authority in Terms of Reference documentation	☐	Negotiation capability with peers	☐
Executive rank – line authority	☐	Ability to build or maintain political alliances	☐
Contract of employment or hiring basis – delegated limits of authority such as cheque-signing authority	☐	The PM's use of their position (e.g. on a strategically essential project)	☐

COACHING SESSION 50

Determine and design your authority

It is important to identify the sorts of things you need to be authorized to carry out or to ask of others. What do you want to have the authority (power and influence) to do? Use the following tick list.

1. Control the master version of the project plan and schedule changes to it. ☐
2. Assign project work package or product priorities. ☐
3. Adjust performance requirements. ☐
4. Monitor financial performance, productivity and change requests. ☐
5. Effect contract changes. ☐
6. Re-allocate project funds. ☐
7. 'Make versus buy' or other lifecycle choice decisions. ☐
8. Initiate support work. ☐
9. Initiate and control configuration changes. ☐
10. Hire subcontractors. ☐
11. Hire additional people. ☐
12. Release people as the project or specialist stage declines or draws to a close. ☐
13. Reward project contributors. ☐
14. Other: ☐

_____

_____

_____

It is equally important to understand and communicate the method by which you will exercise your delegated authority. Use the following tick list.

15. Determining project requirements. ☐
16. Providing organizational and functional mobility. ☐
17. Participating in major decisions. ☐
18. Collaborating in recruiting and staffing the project. ☐
19. Participating in budgeting, funding and scheduling. ☐
20. Selecting the project team. ☐
21. Maintaining the team integrity. ☐
22. Creating and updating project plans. ☐

23. Providing a project management information and reporting system. ☐

24. Designing the project organizational structure and liaison relationships. ☐

25. Serving as the prime contact for stakeholder, customer or client liaison. ☐

Now answer the following questions:

26. What are the tangible differences from this checklist in your environment?

_____

_____

_____

_____

_____

_____

27. How does this benefit your role or cause difficulties?

_____

_____

_____

_____

_____

_____

Office politics are shaped by a number of factors whose negative effects can be eliminated. Which of the following might apply to your situation or environment?

- Imbalanced apportionment of resources causing tribal warfare between teams competing for resources limited by line managers.

- Encouraging competition between people in a climate that encourages people to compete for promotion and its rewards instead of rewarding people for teamwork and collaboration, regardless of how senior they become.

- Imbalanced needs – the needs of the individual, the task and the team/ organization must be balanced such that people do not feel compelled to manipulate matters to satisfy their needs. See Figure 6.1.

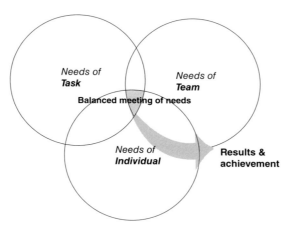

Figure 6.1 Action-Centred Leadership (based on John Adair's three-circle model)

COACHING SESSION 51

Rate your ability as a project leader

The very least of your responsibilities as the project leader is to manage the tasks, the individuals and the team's performance. How do you rate your current ability to do each of the following. Enter 1 for 'poor' increasing to 10 for 'outstanding'.

1. Achieving the task ☐

2. Managing the team or group ☐

3. Managing individuals ☐

4. Record what actions you want to take based on your self-assessment.

_____

_____

_____

_____

_____

_____

_____

_____

_____

_____

_____

_____

_____

_____

_____

_____

_____

_____

_____

Therefore, considering any potential cause for conflict, the political landscape needs to be understood. Political conflict can arise:

- between project managers and line managers
- between project manager and a peer project manager
- between project manager and boss
- between project manager and the customer
- within the project team.

COACHING SESSION 52

Causes of negative project politics

The following is a list of the common causes of negative project politics such as misunderstandings or lack of consensus or agreement. Tick any that apply to your situation.

1. The identity of the final decision-maker is ambiguous. ☐

2. Who the design authority is for the project and its products is unclear or ambiguous. ☐

3. The delegated limits of authority and tasks of the various players are unclear or ambiguous. ☐

4. Conflicting goals and objectives remain unqualified. ☐

The appropriate allocation and use of resources are unclear or ambiguous for the following types of resources:

5. Development and test systems ☐

6. Facilities and accommodation ☐

7. Technical staff ☐

8. Onshore/offshore supply chain ☐

9. Administrative support ☐

10. Business representation ☐

11. Experts ☐

Make notes of what you need to do as thoughts occur to you while completing this checklist:

_____

_____

_____

_____

_____

_____

_____

_____

_____

_____

_____

_____

_____

COACHING SESSION 53

Becoming politically savvy: basic planning principles

Consider Figure 6.2:

Figure 6.2 Becoming politically savvy: basic planning principles (sample)

Recreate this to scope and scale on a flipchart or in a project workbook, as in Figure 6.3:

Figure 6.3 Becoming politically savvy: basic planning principles (template)

Work to identify the **key players** who can help you with resources and project decisions. The other stakeholders can be communicated with as is appropriate to their lesser influence or interest. Consider the people or groups who have some measure of:

- influence over policy and resources

- interest in your organization or project.

Who are the individuals, their key roles or group names for your project?

_____

_____

_____

_____

_____

_____

_____

_____

_____

_____

_____

COACHING SESSION 54

Consequences of negative political behaviours

It is an important part of your development as a PM and agent of change to confront the situation (however private a process that might be) when political behaviours are becoming so extreme that failure to act may result in the most serious of situations. In some extreme cases, the results of unresolved conflict have been:

1. lost customers ☐
2. cancelled contracts ☐
3. failed projects ☐
4. severe loss of talented personnel ☐
5. reputation damage (as in the case of Enron, World Com, Burma Castrol and others) ☐

Tick any that have applied to your organization.

6. For any that you have ticked, describe the consequences and what you would do differently should similar symptoms arise.

_____

_____

_____

_____

_____

_____

_____

_____

_____

_____

POLITICALLY INTELLIGENT THINGS TO DO OR TO AVOID

Be brave and bold in making relationships and networking:

- **Find ways of making relationships with people at all levels** – peer, management, executive. If this is not easy owing to your work structure, then find out about any activities such as any relating to corporate social responsibility (charities, community projects) and see whether you can volunteer. Additionally, you can meet people for social and cultural reasons: food and drink, theatre, cinema, concerts, opera or ballet. Social approaches to senior figures may appear more obvious than when connecting through voluntary work.

- **Do not be afraid of authority figures** – people showing evident signs of fear can make those in authority feel as uncomfortable as people being overly familiar with them. They are just flesh and blood like you. Behave in a way to engender mutual respect and positive regard; avoid empty flattery.

- Get someone you admire to be your **mentor**.

- **Identify and build relationships** with those who you know to be in the informal circle of key personnel.

- Expect there to be **multiple networks** which you have to engage with. For example, your organization may have a natural affiliation with specific industries and professions. Consider attending events and investigate associate or affiliate membership. Alternatively, if the mission of the institute or society is appropriate for your background and career aspirations, consider joining on a qualification or accreditation path and seek a mentor from your organization who can help you.

- While being friendly and engaging with everyone, **try not to ally yourself with any particular cause** and become well versed in the organizational culture and political climate. Even then, have your escape route organized by maintaining transferrable skills and keeping a strong, well-informed network outside your organization.

- **Listen to people four times as much as you speak to them** – people will love you for it; your 'database of what is going on' will rocket in size and scope. Regularly check your understanding of what you have heard when it is appropriate – this shows interest and authenticity.

- **Political intelligence** is the pivotal skillset in stakeholder analysis and management. It is not just about compiling contact information and running weekly facilitated events.

- If you have any experience of the politics turning you from a hero into a heretic, then you'll be drawn towards having greater perception, shrewdness and subtle influence in the workplace.

Things to avoid or do less of:

- **Be cautious how you use information** and do not brag about where you heard things; you will gain access to lots of information and hear of opportunities through your expanded spheres of influence.

- **Practise self-restraint and self-control** with regard to trading on gossip or spreading rumours.

😮😮 COACHING SESSION 55

Identify who is a danger and whom you can help

1. Use any sources of information about questionable decisions or interpersonal conflict very cautiously. Never rush into acting on information of a sensitive nature, it could bite back severely. Avoid complaining publicly. Identify who could be a bad influence in this capacity:

_____

_____

_____

_____

_____

_____

2. Be a good role model for others, showing integrity, keeping your promises and actively discouraging negative politics. Identify whom you think you can help:

_____

_____

_____

_____

_____

_____

_____

_____

'One of the penalties of refusing to participate in politics is that you end up being governed by your inferiors.'

Plato

 NEXT STEPS

This chapter commenced with assessments and guidance with follow-on exercises to help you gain a deeper understanding of your current political situation and how to handle it. A political agenda may put a personal slant on an established change agenda and agreed project purpose, giving it a spin to more closely match the needs or aspirations of a group of stakeholders. The next chapter goes into stakeholder management in more depth, helping you to become more astute in managing the politics associated with your role.

TAKEAWAYS

Explain why a PM has to understand the impact of politics as a change agent.

_____

_____

_____

_____

_____

_____

_____

_____

_____

_____

Identify the potential sources of your authority.

_____

_____

_____

_____

_____

_____

_____

_____

_____

_____

_____

_____

Identify the responsibilities that the Action-Centred Leadership model implies belong to a PM.

_____

_____

_____

_____

_____

_____

_____

_____

_____

List the politically intelligent things you plan to do as a result of identifying with statements in this chapter.

_____

_____

_____

_____

_____

_____

_____

_____

_____

_____

_____

STAKEHOLDER MANAGEMENT

OBJECTIVES FOR THIS CHAPTER

- Understand what stakeholders are.
- Understand why we need to manage stakeholders.
- Devise a strategy to inculcate stakeholders into the project's design.
- Understand stakeholders' interests and impact and what you can do about these.
- Consider the most appropriate means to influence key players and how they can be positively influenced to improve the success of the project and thereby their relevant relationships.

These are challenging times for us all at work; there's pressure on the way we work together and how we manage change. Engaging stakeholders and managing the outcomes are a vital aspect of concluding a project as a financially viable business venture without which PMs are unlikely to succeed. Stakeholder management is a lengthy responsibility covering not just the life of the project but the life of the products or outcomes of the project as well. A significant and inescapable management responsibility is estimating the costs and ensuring that the benefits outweigh them as soon as is feasible in the life of the project's outputs. This chapter introduces a range of techniques for you to contextualize and to produce valuable and pertinent outputs.

This chapter uses preceding work to cope with more complexity. It especially uses the understanding gained on communications planning and about handling politics, helping you to become more astute about the business outcome and project mission.

WHAT ARE PROJECT STAKEHOLDERS?

Stakeholders are people with an investment or interest in delivering part or all of the project and its outcomes, or are people who are to adopt those outputs as new ways of working or as part of their product portfolio. It is worth knowing that:

- More people than you might think have their lives touched by projects: about £10 ($16.4) trillion – one-quarter of the globe's annual gross product – is spent on projects – motivation enough for effectively managing stakeholders.

- There are at least 2 million project, programme and portfolio-level practitioners in the UK alone; most large organizations have pools of change managers responsible for stakeholder engagement.

It is vital for a PM to create engagement with stakeholders:

- Influence needs to be engendered by personal communication.

- Engagement requires intelligent research and planning.

- Engagement means handling politics as well as by using the influencing skills and strategies explored in earlier chapters.

However, we'll look at stakeholder management from both the change agent and the 'business as usual' perspectives (i.e. the customers of change programmes). We'll explore the processes that these change agents need to follow as well as alternative strategies to match unique contexts. If you do not have official delegated lines of authority over money and people such as in a matrix management situation, then you can become a person seen as influential through developing your expertise, providing evidence to justify your resource needs, providing sources of information and strengthening your connections.

This chapter helps you gather, focus or reprioritize the information you need to decide your tactics and approaches based on what you now know is the situation (i.e. the legitimate change agenda versus emerging political agendas; key relationships and their allegiances; any vulnerable groups and allies on whom you can rely to progress towards beneficial outcomes for the project).

WHY DO WE NEED TO MANAGE STAKEHOLDERS?

Change impacts people pervasively and the greater the number of people, the more likely it is that your actions will affect those with power and influence over project goals. Remember that, by managing stakeholders using a communications strategy with more subtle and astute influence, you also make yourself less vulnerable to power exercised by those (hopefully few) senior stakeholders operating hierarchically on a political agenda which slows, hijacks or hampers change.

The benefits of using a stakeholder-based approach are that you can use the opinions of the most powerful to shape your project at an early stage. Stakeholders' involvement makes it more likely that you will succeed, while the challenges they set and the support they give can also improve project quality.

COACH'S TIP

Communicate with your stakeholders

By communicating with stakeholders early and frequently, you can ensure that they fully understand what you are doing and the benefits of your project; they can actively support you when necessary.

A common reason why an IT project fails is due, not to the technology, but to people not being brought together to create and support the project. Much is made of the important need to engage with staff and win their support; equally, however, it is necessary to win the support of all types of stakeholder and interested parties.

You can also provide evidence that a comprehensive set of interested parties have been considered and consulted. These people could be backers or blockers. Stakeholders are made up of:

- those who **make** it happen
- those who **watch** it happen
- those who **wonder** what happened!

In this chapter you will find further fact-gathering and intelligence-gathering exercises whose results should be set up as a project database or filing structure.

The following factors need to be considered in winning the support of those with vested interests in the project:

- Is the **'capability maturity model'** relevant?
    - How mature is your organization?
    - What is the impact of your level of maturity on the likely success of the change project?
    - What are the transitions required to higher maturity?

- Are there **legal issues** preventing or driving the need for change?

- **Communications** – have you the skills required in crafting messages to match the stakeholders' profile in terms of frequency, timeliness, channel, content of announcements and linkage to events?

- **Coaching and development** – do you have a continuum of learning active in the workplace?

  - Individual development budget – what is affordable to engender the type of change required?

  - Leadership and management styles appropriate to type of programme and pace of change.

  - Personal development (stretching competence to build discriminating competence) versus project delivery (risk to quality or deadlines) when allocating tasks in your team and engaging stakeholders in activities.

  - Performance management – remember the Introduction's commentary about triple-loop learning – are we measuring the right thing and measuring it right? How do we decide what is right for us?

  - Team motivation and development – are staff actively engaged with the change action plan?

  - Professional issues, ethics, code of conduct, etc.

At each stage, the change organization needs good management information on:

- all likely emotional responses to the intended change

- what the implementation involves

- what messages have been disseminated and to whom

- which external sources of communication are affecting reputation

- which sources of communication might affect your ability to continue the programme.

Stakeholder analysis is the technique used to identify the key people who have to be won over. You can predict people's reactions to your project and build into your plan the actions that will win people's support. You need to understand the impact, positive or negative, that stakeholders can have on the progress and outcomes of the project – as illustrated in Figure 7.1.

Stakeholder planning is used to grow the support that helps you succeed. Gaining support from powerful stakeholders can help you to win more resources – this makes it more likely that your projects will be successful.

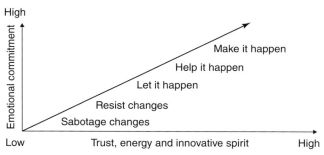

Figure 7.1 Leading transitions

You need to craft messages to the right people, at the right frequency, at the appropriate level of detail and tuned to their interests and accountabilities. Hence the work that goes into the communications plan is highly beneficial to your team, smoothing the path for the products of your team's work when the outputs 'go live'.

Stakeholder management is an important discipline that successful people use to win support from others. It helps them ensure that their projects succeed where others fail. Chapter 9 picks up this activity as a collaborative one with your sponsor and other key relationships. By communicating with stakeholders early and frequently, you can ensure that they fully understand what you are doing and the benefits of your project; they can actively support you when necessary.

As Figure 7.1 illustrates, in leading stakeholders through transitions you will find that stakeholders can be divided into:

- those who want to **make** it happen (trustworthy, proactive, energetic, emotionally committed, innovative, assertive, actively engaged)
- those who will **help** it happen (active, committed, willing)
- those who will **let** it happen (passive or passive aggressive, laissez-faire).
- those who **wonder** what happened! (i.e. passive or not actively engaged in the process)
- those who **want it stopped** or impeded (politically active, actively aggressive saboteurs).

You need to take all these attitudes to the change agenda into account. Resistance is costly and often nugatory, whereas it may not take much to motivate the 'let it happen' demographic and get them further up the commitment scales.

COACHING SESSION 56

Identify the stakeholder demographics

Identify the tipping point for your project between the effort needed to create a majority in favour of the change happening in comparison to converting or neutralizing the percentage who want to actively sabotage or resist changes. Make notes here on your ideas (survey, focus group, representatives):

_____

_____

_____

_____

_____

_____

_____

_____

_____

_____

_____

_____

HOW TO CONDUCT A STAKEHOLDER ANALYSIS

COACHING SESSION 57

Stakeholder audience analysis and plan

Create your own initial stakeholder audience analysis using the template (Figure 7.2; expanded as you see fit) or adapt it to your own needs and ideas. Some of the cells are filled in with typical content. If you are managing a small project, you may find that this exercise covers most of what is required and no further analysis is necessary. The communication plan can be further developed as the project progresses into an integrated communications strategy with multiple campaign plans.

Project: _____

Purpose: _____

Stakeholder	Outline communications objective	Audience motivation or perspective	Messages	Approach/Media or channels	Allocated activity to (contact details)	Timing	Priority	Feedback cycle	Managed by:
Population to be influenced	A well-formed outcome	Emotional legacy?	Value proposition or offer	Modern social media implies a pull approach not a push strategy (sell)	Who will implement it?			Run a pilot?	
		Towards motivator: Attracted to a reward?		Face to face or notice boards and printed matter				Survey?	
		Away from: Repelled from a consequence?						Routine meeting?	

Figure 7.2 Stakeholder analysis plan

You may also find it useful to create another table (Figure 7.3) which names stakeholders and analyses their interest, impact, importance and influence as they affect or are affected by the project through a number of steps.

Stakeholder ID group/name	Interests	Impact	Importance/Influence

Figure 7.3 Identifying stakeholders

- **Identity** Name each stakeholder group with a meaningful designation. You need a comprehensive list of all potential beneficiaries (so you know 'what's in it for me' for each stakeholder listed).

- **Interests** You need to understand their interests and expectations on the outcome of the project – this could be a covert political agenda, not an agreed and open change agenda. Record any stakeholder interests which conflict with a goal of the project or its products.

- **Impact** Identify their political sway, social influence, budgetary control or influence through some aspect of diversity (e.g. representing a minority group's interests or union), legal compliance, or control of resources.

  - Who has common interests with you and positions of influence or opportunities?

- Whom can you enrol to help you monitor and control adversaries and to manage 'bedfellows'?

- Identify how organized opponents are as well as supporters.

- Identify anyone who might be adversely affected by the outcome. Who are the vulnerable groups (e.g. old people, disabled people, poor people, people living in a particular geographical region) or those are who are impacted by interim deliverables happening before the end goal.

■ **Importance** What are the relationships among the beneficiaries and vulnerable groups – can you define who knows whom?

■ **Influence** What influencing strategies do you need to persuade them in the direction that you need, to improve the number of allies, to change the mind of opponents or to minimize the negative impact on their relevant relationships? Involvement might create 'buy-in' from stakeholder groups. This may necessitate assimilating stakeholders into designing the project or by participating in further analysis, planning, mapping, engagement and by defining any benefit attainment ownership and accountabilities (i.e. bringing in a saving or cost avoidance benefit).

COACH'S TIP

Find out and record all stakeholders' key meetings to add the communications plan calendar.

Figure 7.4 can also help you to choose the type of communication that you will have with stakeholders:

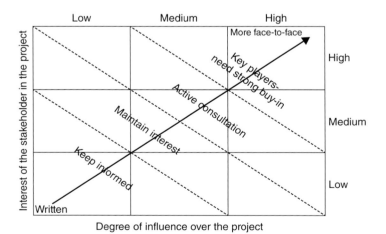

Figure 7.4 Level of communication/contact with stakeholders

For example, those key players who have high influence and high interest in the outcome of the project need more face-to-face contact from your sponsor (and you, as appropriate). Those with low interest and low influence may receive written (or web-based) communications, as they simply need to be kept informed of progress to make sure that expectations do not drift away from what will be delivered.

Examine the most affordable communication strategy by using what is already a potential channel or media. Use free or low-cost channels, too. Find out which channel reaches which demographic of stakeholders. Apply the 80/20 rule to get best value where feasible. The communication plan can be further developed as the project progresses into an integrated communications strategy with multiple campaign plans.

THREE-DIMENSIONAL VIEW OF STAKEHOLDER POWER, INTEREST AND ATTITUDE

The following diagnostic tool (in Coaching session 58) offers an alternative, 'under the table' understanding of a stakeholder's power. Whereas the table in Coaching session 57 above shows a 2D view, this potent assessment tool offers a 3D view of a stakeholder's power, interest and attitude to the goals and outcomes of your project:

- **Power** Are the holders of power relevant to the project? Are they *influential* or *insignificant* in terms of authority?

- **Interest** Are they interested in the project in that they will be *active* in it? Will they take a *passive* role in the project due to lack of interest, and will their business areas be impacted by it?

- **Attitude** Are they backers or blockers?

Using this diagnostic tool should make it more obvious 'whom you have to stop doing what' and 'whom you have to persuade to be active in a positive way'.

ᑐᑐ COACHING SESSION 58

Stakeholder power: the three-dimensional view

Use this table to help you evaluate the best approach to building stakeholder engagement. You can add more details of issues, messages, activities/action, key lead person and dates as required.

Stakeholder name	Assessment – Are they influential or not?	Power	Interest	Attitude	Pseudonym	Your decision on how to handle
	Influential	High	Active	Backer	Saviour	Enlist!
	↓	High	Passive	Backer	Sleeping giant	Alarm call!
	↓	High	Active	Blocker	Saboteur	Neutralize
	↓	High	Passive	Blocker	Time bomb	Bargain with?
	↓	Low	Active	Backer	Friend	Sounding board
	↓	Low	Active	Blocker	Irritant	Neutralize
	↓	Low	Passive	Backer	Acquaintance	Keep informed
	Insignificant	Low	Passive	Blocker	Trip wire	Neutralize

A PM should think carefully about stakeholders who are identified as powerful and positive to the project but passive in terms of activity (the 'sleeping giants'). How useful is that to you or your sponsor? What can you do to make powerful backers more active in the most beneficial way? This is valuable information if you and your sponsor are willing to sound out your assumptions and are prepared to change your mind about people's power, interest and attitude.

In this chapter there have been many matrixes (tables) which have 'stakeholder' as the first column. Building on the '2D' table where you identified interests and potential impact, you can now map the political allegiances and their relative positions – whether they are allies, opponents or neutrals. The template in Coaching session 59 (Figure 7.5) is a simple but powerful tool which illustrates allegiances in a visual way:

- **Allies** In this instance, there is both high agreement and high trust between you and an ally. You have open communication, share concerns or opinions, and feel authentic in their company. Around allies, it's OK to feel vulnerable as they will not take advantage of it. You feel support flowing spontaneously, easily and naturally. Identify and use their strengths and connections.

- **Opponents** Someone is your opponent because they are genuinely in disagreement with you on a point, goal or ambition. They can be trusted to overtly communicate their reasons for not supporting your vision, purpose, direction or goals. There is no deceit.

- **Bedfellows** These are people whom you need to be careful around because they appear to agree but you do not trust them for some reason. You might want to carefully craft communications with them, not exposing as much information as you would to your allies.

- **Fence-sitters** You are likely to have insufficient information to know to what degree to trust these people or to express the level of agreement between you that exists on your vision, purpose, direction or goals. Low trust and unknown agreement characterizes your view of them.

- **Adversaries** These types may well have been a bedfellow at some point but they have switched sides or become hard to pin down. Anticipate that they will not support your vision, purpose, direction or goals. Expect them to soak up time and energy as they try to sabotage your plans. You must prioritize collaborating with allies to manage or neutralize adversaries.

 COACHING SESSION 59

Visualize your stakeholders

Figure 7.5 is a way of visualizing the answers you have in the 'Identifying stakeholders' table above (Figure 7.3) and builds on the previous analyses; the information extracted identifies whom you can influence to achieve your end goals.

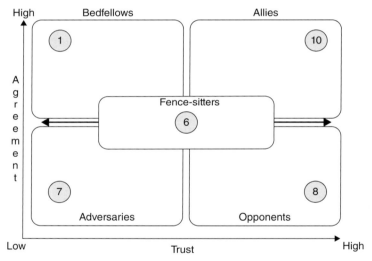

Figure 7.5 Template for visualizing your stakeholders

! **COACH'S TIP**

Get to know your stakeholders

You will have to make the effort to get to know people and their work on a professional basis and grow trust with them first before confirming agreement. What is the bond between or among the key relationships identified? Keep this information private and confidential.

LINKING IN THE PROJECT STAGES TO GET A TIMELINE

At each stage, the change organization needs good management information on:

- all likely emotional responses to the intended change
- what the implementation involves
- what messages have been disseminated and to whom
- which external sources of communication are affecting reputation
- which sources of communication might affect your ability to continue the programme.

The majority of this information will be gleaned through relationship skills.

You need to integrate the timing of technical products which emerge in each stage of the project with what else is happening to the stakeholders in the wider business. In this way, the 'business as usual' activity is related to the project schedule. If you do not achieve this, then carefully crafted messages can get lost in the 'white noise' of business life; people suffer from information overload all too commonly these days and your efforts will be uncoordinated and useless. In other words, you need to expand or clarify the project calendar.

Map out how the stakeholders should be involved and at which stage of the project using your stakeholder tables and map of allies and other allegiances. Use the table below (in Coaching session 60) to relate project stages with different types of participation in project events and communications activities. This results in a sense of timing and sequence in overall planning. Assess the relative point of impact in project stages and how this affects their importance; reorder the list when you have completed this so that it's prioritized and in order of urgency.

Plan stakeholders' involvement stage by stage, taking into account their interests, their likely ability to impact the project (scope, budget, risks, quality) and their relationships (formal, informal).

Identify one or more forms of participation which suits their capabilities and availability to keep them actively engaged in beneficial ways to the project goals. Examples are focus groups, requirements-gathering interviews, 'show and tell' events (when you have sufficient code to demonstrate functionality), or gateway events.

 COACH'S TIP

Remember...

You need to craft messages to the right people, at the right frequency (daily, weekly, monthly, stage-ends) and at the appropriate level of detail, tuned to their interests and accountabilities. This was documented in the end-to-end communication plan introduced in Chapter 5.

COACHING SESSION 60

Integrate stakeholders into your project timeline

Create a table or series of flipcharts which map out all the information collected. It should look something like this:

Project stages (examples only – add your own)	Type of participation				
	1	2	3	4	5
1 Start-up					
2 Formation					
3 Definition					
4 Joint diagnosis/ mobilization					
5 Main build					
6 Delivery and handover					
7 Review and 'next steps'					

NEXT STEPS

This chapter has built on all the analysis work to date but especially on the understanding gained in Chapter 5 in communications planning and about handling politics in Chapter 6, which helped you to become more astute in your role and about the project mission. In this chapter you learned why we need to manage stakeholders, by going into stakeholder management in more depth and introducing a range of skills and techniques for you to contextualize and to produce valuable and pertinent outputs.

Following on from here, in Chapter 8 we will examine your relationship with your sponsor in more depth and look at how to help the customer journey run more smoothly.

TAKEAWAYS

Why do we need to manage stakeholders?

_____

_____

_____

_____

_____

_____

How can you identify the stakeholders and understand their interests and impact?

_____

_____

_____

_____

_____

_____

_____

_____

_____

How do you manage each group?

• Those who want to make it happen.

_____

_____

_____

_____

_____

_____

- Those who will watch it happen.

  _____

  _____

  _____

  _____

- Those who wonder what happened.

  _____

  _____

  _____

  _____

- Those who want it stopped or impeded.

  _____

  _____

  _____

  _____

What factors do you need to take into account in order to devise the most appropriate means to influence stakeholders and thus their relevant relationships.

_____

_____

_____

_____

_____

_____

_____

_____

_____

MOBILIZING CHANGE

8

 OUTCOMES FROM THIS CHAPTER

- Understand change readiness as a concept which differs from change management and understand the role of the change leader.
- Undertake assessments of your current ability to cope with change and of your organization's current ability to cope with change.
- Understand how human beings process significant changes or upheavals.
- Learn a technique which specialists use to explore and mobilize change.
- Develop an integrated approach to communications and change.

This chapter introduces techniques designed to engage individuals, groups and the organization in exploring the nature of a change and a future state. PMs need to understand how people become mobilized and in this chapter various techniques for activating change in people are explained. People can be in a 'comfort zone' which holds a project back from progressing or leads to a rejection or ambivalence about its goals.

CHANGE READINESS AUDIT

> *'Luck happens when preparation meets opportunity!'*

Best practice for change is about being 'change ready', where the current organizational culture, co-operation among individuals and leadership are aligned with the change direction and as enablers for a successful change process.

One of the key lessons of this workbook is that, if there were more emphasis on individuals, groups and organizations being 'change ready' or 'fit for change', combined with more effective change management (portfolio, programme and project management practice), then there would be fewer failed initiatives. More focus on mindfulness, attitudes and agility (i.e. change readiness) and less on doctrine and methodology (change management) would serve us well.

In this chapter you will take part in two coaching sessions (assessments) which will allow you to consider whether there is a discrepancy between change readiness and change management in your experience.

Change readiness is about assessing the willingness of your people to embark upon a specific programme of changes which will enable an organization to move from where it is now to where it needs to get to. Before you can improve your change readiness, you must first assess the current change awareness, agility, reactions and mechanisms.

With the passage of time, organizations establish a set of 'rules' by which they operate; as we know, we would normally refer to these as the 'culture' of an organization – that is, 'the way we do things around here'. These rules are all well and good in stable environments, but when change is driven by external factors such as global financial instability, recession and/or turbulent market forces, then the effect upon any organization is to destabilize it. So we have to take positive and early action to ensure our ability to:

- survive turbulent times
- prepare for emergence from such turbulent times.

A key element of taking positive early action is to conduct a change readiness audit. Remember that the audit should be applied to key external stakeholders as well as to a fully representative sample of your people. Such an audit (which you would need to adapt to fit your specific needs) should address the following topics:

- the current state (as is)
- strategic change drivers (the causes and the drivers of the strategic change)
- the future state (the vision of what's to be).
- a change analysis matrix (an analysis of the constituent characteristics of projects within the overall programme)
- a change impact matrix (systems thinking applied across the organization)
- climate and culture (the working environment – 'how we do things around here')
- leading the change (leadership and change champion)
- the change architecture (determination of key stakeholders, interaction and the decision-making processes)
- communications (planning and implementation)
- performance management (how you will monitor progress and integrate with 'business as usual').

To specify all of these would be a book on its own and it is not feasible to cover all of them here (they would need in any case to be heavily contextualized to fit your circumstances, industry, degree of organizational maturity and current PESTLE status). However, this chapter has two assessments – which can be completed by you and/or used with others, too. The first is a self-assessment of your current ability to cope with change and the second is the organization's.

COACHING SESSION 61

Self-assessment: your current ability to cope with change

1. Write down how you feel about change.

_____

_____

_____

_____

_____

_____

2. Why might you not like change?

_____

_____

_____

_____

_____

_____

3. Do you have any specific goals (e.g. wanting to change personally or get a new job)?

_____

_____

_____

_____

_____

4. Do you need more time to do things that you want to do?

_____

_____

5. Have you got any overall sense of direction?

6. Do you know what you do not want to do?

Do you want to improve relationships at work or in the home? Think of situations where you have had to deal with change and assess your track record in dealing with it. Try to think of at least one change in each category.

7. A change at **home** over which I had **no** control:

8. A change at **work** over which I had **no** control:

_____

_____

_____

_____

_____

9. A change at **home** over which I had **some** control:

_____

_____

_____

_____

_____

_____

10. A change at **work** over which I had **some** control:

_____

_____

_____

_____

_____

_____

Look back over the four situations that you have described and see whether there are patterns in how you have dealt with them.

11. When faced with change that I have **no** control over, I usually respond by:

_____

_____

_____

_____

12. When faced with change that I have **some** control over, I usually respond by:

13. When dealing with change, the things I do well are:

14. The differences between the ways I deal with change at work and at home are:

Over the next day or two telephone someone who knows you well and ask them: 'In your opinion, how do I cope with change?'

15. Jot down their reply here:

_____

_____

_____

_____

_____

_____

16. How do their views compare with yours?

_____

_____

_____

_____

_____

Having added external feedback to your own self-assessment, is there a difference between change at home and work? Perhaps others see that you cope better than you think you do?

17. What can you learn from the feedback that you have received?

_____

_____

_____

_____

_____

_____

18. What pattern of coping do you have with change? Tick all that apply:

Pretend that it is not happening ☐

Insist that the old way is better/safer ☐

Accept it once someone else has made the effort to change your mind ☐

Immediately accept it at face value because it's new ☐

Initiate the change yourself to control it ☐

Thrive on it! ☐

Other:

_____

_____

_____

19. Having added external feedback to your own self-assessment, do you want to change anything about yourself? If so, how or what?

_____

_____

_____

_____

_____

_____

_____

20. Write down how you are feeling about all this now? Tick which of the following applies to you:

Impatient to start ☐

Wishing you had never decided to do this ☐

Anxious ☐

Ready to make changes ☐

Other:

_____

_____

_____

_____

_____

_____

_____

In this section, you have found out about your personal responses to change. Create a personal resource log and put down the points that you want to remember about your response to change. What actions will you now take to make a start in developing yourself to your full potential?

I will by [date...]

COACHING SESSION 62

Assessment: your organization's track record with change

1. Does your organization have the agility and flexibility to change?

_____

_____

_____

_____

_____

_____

2. Would you assess the current organizational culture, co-operation among individuals and leadership to be aligned with the change direction and as enablers for a successful change process?

_____

_____

_____

_____

_____

3. Are you aware of external change drivers – that is, can you write about each of the following: Political, Economic, Sociological, Technological, Legal and Environmental (PESTLE)?

_____

_____

_____

_____

_____

4. What internally driven needs to change ('people factors') exist at present?

_____

_____

_____

_____

_____

5. Are people willing to engage with potential changes and explore what the future state may be like for them?

_____

_____

_____

_____

_____

6. What is the extent of the culture gap between the 'as is' current state and 'to be' future state (desired versus current culture)?

_____

_____

_____

_____

7. Do your leaders recognize that the steady state rarely exists now?

_____

_____

_____

_____

_____

8. Do your change mechanisms encourage clear goal alignment across functions?

_____

_____

_____

_____

_____

9. How good is your ability to integrate a change into existing systems?

_____

_____

_____

_____

_____

10. How are people accountable for results?

_____

_____

_____

_____

_____

11. Do your reward systems reinforce desired change behaviours?

_____

_____

_____

_____

12. Are your change mechanisms sufficiently contextualized to allow change without disruption to current business operations?

13. Are your structures and systems flexible enough to adapt and support the implementation of change?

14. Does your organization have the structures and systems in place to support the successful implementation of change?

15. Do you understand the difference between change readiness and change management?

_____

_____

_____

_____

_____

_____

In summary, change mechanisms should encourage clear goal alignment across functions, enabling integration of a change into existing systems, have unchallenged accountability for results, and reward systems that reinforce desired change behaviours. This contextual focus is critical to the ability to implement desired change with no interruption to daily operation ('business as usual'). Are your structures and systems flexible enough to adapt and support the implementation of change? Does your organization have the structures and systems in place to support the successful implementation of change?

Add your thoughts regarding this summary and how it applies to your organization in the space provided.

_____

_____

_____

_____

_____

_____

_____

_____

_____

_____

_____

THE ELISABETH KÜBLER-ROSS CHANGE CURVE

'Change can be beneficial if managed correctly because it can help staff clear lots of things up that have been holding them back. As a manager you give them the skills to move on; you don't tell them to move on, you enable them to move on.'

Fiona Willmot, Head of Relationship Team, Skills Funding Agency

According to Elisabeth Kübler-Ross's theory, human beings process significant changes or upheavals in a similar way to bereavement – there is a sense of personal loss; something that was expected will now never be. The Kübler-Ross Change Curve (see Figure 8.1) describes the roller-coaster of emotions that occur when we receive a shock which causes us to grieve for someone, for a past state of affairs or due to unmet expectations owing to change(s) beyond our control. The graph identifies the stages that everyone moves through at different rates (it is possible to move backwards a bit, too, but eventually we do move through all the stages).

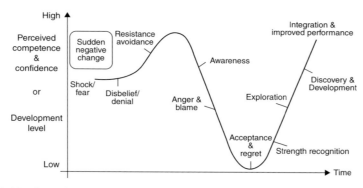

Figure 8.1 The Kübler-Ross Change Curve

In a project, when business users or customers take on-board the impact of business changes for them, they may appear to be in shock or denial. As a change agent, you need to be aware how their behaviour manifests itself as they go through this process:

■ They may perceive some sort of deficit or loss in their role, standing, promotion prospects, pay and rewards, or other aspects of being an employee.

■ Self-confidence is knocked by the change and it is important that support is high to make the dip in confidence as short as possible.

- Given time and the opportunity to share conflicting thoughts, emotions and memories, people develop the ability to absorb the change and to move on to a new life.

The following is a slightly elongated version of Elisabeth Kübler-Ross's original five-step model:

Kübler-Ross stage	Meaning
Stage 1 – Shock/fear	'I don't believe it!' Surprise or trauma in response. 'Isn't it awful?' 'I do not believe it has happened.' 'What will happen to me now?'
Stage 2 – Disbelief or denial	The change is shut out, denied or rejected and ways are found to prove that it isn't happening. 'It cannot be real or true.'
Stage 3 – Resistance, avoidance and frustration	Falling out of denial and into depression but experiencing anger and frustration. Trends are to lash out, be judgemental, blame others; still no acceptance of the change; adoption of a victim or martyr role: 'Why me?'
Stage 4 – Rock bottom Regret acceptance	Apathy and depression follow; person hits rock-bottom. Everything is pointless; therefore there is no mileage in doing anything. There is a lack of self-confidence. 'I'm ready to give up.' 'I don't care.'
Stage 5 – Experiment, recognition, exploration	The previous stage is so depressing that most people pull themselves out of it – this is where you will start to try out new things. Anything is better than Stage 4 so: 'I will try this.'
Stage 6 – Decision time – discovery and development	Deciding what does and does not work. At this stage, the change is accepted and this leads to the person feeling better, more optimistic and enthusiastic. 'This is not so bad after all – it actually seems to be working!'
Stage 7 – Integration improved performance	Integrating means making the change transition into a norm for you (i.e. 'The new me'). It means that the person has accepted the change, assimilating its impact on your previous routine and putting together something that works for you now.

COACHING SESSION 63

You, your team and the Kübler-Ross Change Curve

Take a look at the Kübler-Ross Change Curve to see whether any of your reactions to change fit. If you are a person who thinks more about the past, it is likely that you will get stuck in feeling depressed and then slip back into the denial stage. If you are more forward-looking, you may always be trying out new ideas without ever actually moving on to integrate them. Most people have difficulty moving between the fifth, sixth and seventh stages.

1. Where is your particular danger point?

_____

_____

_____

_____

_____

_____

_____

2. Use your reflections to assess your project team. How would team members cope with intended change (you may need them to relocate; change development methodology; work with a different supplier; accept sharing of resources that they previously had to themselves).

_____

_____

_____

_____

_____

_____

_____

3. Think about the different stakeholder groups and the broader community in your project, programme and portfolio. What are they facing?

_____

_____

_____

_____

_____

_____

_____

4. How do you think they will react?

_____

_____

_____

_____

_____

_____

_____

5. What can you learn from this chapter which will help them to cope well?

_____

_____

_____

_____

_____

_____

_____

It is heart-warming to know that we humans all have this process in common. By reaching out to one other, we have the opportunity to emerge as bonded (through sharing) and integrated adults from a joint process. The change curve is useful to understand because it stems from our evolution where it has allowed us to adapt to changes in our environment imposed on us. Without this mechanism, we may have died out as a species many millennia ago.

Riding this roller-coaster is not a pleasant experience. However, it can lead to a greater state of happiness and wellbeing than we have ever achieved before (i.e. a successful adaptation). Because humans have free will, it is an individual process where our thoughts, actions, awareness and self-control play a part in how quickly we move through to the end of the curve.

If we consciously work through the curve, creating for ourselves a story that leads us to its successful conclusion, we have hope and do not fear the future. This is where Beckhard's Formula for Change can play a part.

BECKHARD'S FORMULA FOR CHANGE

According to a long-established change equation by Richard Beckhard (Figure 8.2), three factors must be present for meaningful organizational change to take place. It is a technique which many occupational psychologists and organizational development specialists use to explore and mobilize change. This has been adapted many times by major consultancies – the letters may change, but the logic is essentially the same.

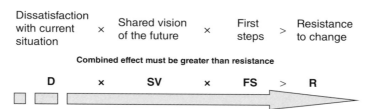

Figure 8.2 Beckhard's Formula for Change

These factors are:

D = **Dissatisfaction** with how things are now

V = **Vision** of what is possible

F = **First**, concrete **steps** that can be taken towards the vision.

Change is possible if the product of these three factors is greater than:

R = **Resistance** to change.

Because D, V, and F are multiplied, if any one of them is absent or low, then the sum product will be low, and therefore overcoming resistance is infeasible.

D = Dissatisfaction with how things are now – if staff are too comfortable or apathetic about work and not actively engaged in their role and responsibilities, then they have inertia holding them back from making a shift.

V = Vision of what is possible – staff need to obtain a model of the future state and see their role in it as an appealing one. Without a sense of being drawn away from the current and towards a vision of the future, the status quo prevails.

F = First steps in the process of change – a change strategy has to have achievable steps to mobilize any shift at all. Often a common reason for failure to change is making these steps too large. You have to be kind to yourself, your team and your organization, and make these steps realistic to be successful.

Beckhard's Formula for Change is a useful model to guide our approach to mobilizing change in individuals, summarized as follows:

1. **Increasing readiness for change** Show limitations of the present. This helps the person to see the problems, accept them and own them.

2. **Build vision of the future** This helps the person to see a more satisfactory future state.

3. The combination of **awareness** raised by 1 and 2 above creates tension which shakes the individual out of their comfort zone.

4. This creates a **drive** to reach a satisfactory state.

5. The **degree of success or rejection** of the new change depends on a person's perceived security and their perception of the probability of the change being a success.

Let's explore the model from left to right. In doing so, we need to be aware that, if any one of the elements to the left of the 'greater than' symbol – > – is omitted, then there will be no reduction in resistance to change; we need to complete each of the elements successfully.

Show limitations of the present

In order to stimulate a change to the status quo, we have to raise levels of dissatisfaction with the current situation. This feels counter-intuitive for managers who normally keep staff satisfaction high. While happy staff is a good thing generally, when needing to meet increasing demand staff must be taken out of their comfort zone by engaging people in a debate about greater opportunities, or about current difficulties and what general dis-satisfiers exist within the present operation. You could use Herzberg's dis-satisfiers here where the model suggested a number of 'hygiene factors' which are strong determiners of job satisfaction:

- achievement
- recognition
- the work itself
- responsibility
- advancement.

By inference, the lack of any of these can be a cause of dissatisfaction.

Shared vision of the future

The vision of the future may be set at the top and cascaded throughout the organization. The vision must be compelling, inspiring and attractive to the majority of employees, and staff must be able to see the transition path clearly and understand their place within it. If they are not to be a part of the new organization, then they must be confident that their moving on will be handled with compassion, honesty and fairness within published legal processes. We'll look more closely at this later. Change readiness is the ability to continuously initiate and respond to change in ways that create advantage, minimize risk, and sustain performance. This continuous and integrated approach to change requires the co-ordinated participation of everyone in the company, not just a few change agents or change leaders.

 COACH'S TIP

Our vision of the future

Our vision needs to establish the goals to which we aspire and the path towards them. It needs to describe the desired state and paint a picture of the future.

Initial steps

It's vitally important to establish achievable and not too ambitious first steps from where you are now to where you want to be in the future. These first steps must engage the entire workforce and should achieve some 'quick wins' that will encourage and incentivize staff to keep going. This becomes feasible by developing and sticking to an action plan which breaks the process down into bite-sized chunks.

The action plan will be the basis of a transitions map which will need to be tailored to your specific circumstances, but generally it should address items such as:

- current situation
- the vision and the future structure
- the barriers to progress
- the capacity for change as well as running the business
- future capability statement and culture description
- required knowledge, skills realignment and learning/coaching skills
- resource and manpower management
- new practitioners' networks, communities of practice.

The action plan to overcome resistance will clearly map the pathway from beginning to end, with both progress being displayed and deviations highlighted and explained. In the process of assessing capability maturity and developing a transitions map, resistance to change should have been tempered and the workforce engaged throughout. This activity is integrated with the communications calendar and plan in Chapter 5. Thus, resistance to change is less than the appetite to deliver the shared vision and to take the first and subsequent steps towards the beneficial change state.

THE CHANGE WHEEL – AN INTEGRATED APPROACH

The following model (Figure 8.3) was developed in conjunction with a banking executive when we commenced work on the merger of two banks with branches on 25 Caribbean islands. I call the model 'the Change Wheel' as it identifies a whole series of interrelated activities and themes:

- top management leadership behaviours
- clarity of purpose and communication (covered in Chapter 5)
- knowledge sharing (discussed in Chapters 5, 10 and 11)
- effective interface through trusting relationships and good-quality interpersonal communication.

Most of these themes require good communication skills, active listening, questioning/probing, dealing with ambiguity, and high emotional intelligence. Let's look at each theme in turn.

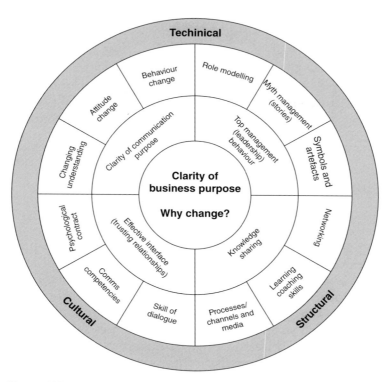

Figure 8.3 The Change Wheel

Top leadership

The top team needs to become greater than the sum of its parts, speaking with one voice and supporting each other by developing the resolve and skills to lead major change. They must establish a clear strategic direction and determine an agreed leadership philosophy. As good role models, they should deal with misaligned stories or myths about past or present change initiatives and strategic ambitions which (unmanaged) may have a negative impact, and recognize that culture is essentially associated with values, beliefs and expectations. Leaders must be sensitive to the attachment staff can have to previous cultural symbols and artefacts (which include logos, brand colours, uniforms, dress style, interior decor and design). They must identify which behaviours are to be rewarded and which should be discouraged. It is important to consciously have more than one leadership style, moving fluidly from a more directive style to a more supportive kind to get better results. This requires self-awareness and self-regulation when dealing with colleagues under pressure. Social awareness, influencing and the ability to transition others through change impacts are equally valuable. Succession plans provide crucial continuity.

Clarity of purpose and communication

A clear leadership agenda must be constructed and plans aligned, including nurturing a broad leadership community. Leaders and specialists need skills to craft the message to engender attitudinal changes and behavioural norms to match a new culture. Patterns of behaviour and the artefacts are the visible symbols of culture. Outdated artefacts can create barriers to change if employees associate with previous behaviours or standards.

Knowledge sharing

Leaders need to develop a deep resolve to lead through when individuals feel insecure, as they do when going through change. All managers from supervisor through to top management must commit to develop the underpinning skills of effective, cohesive and authentic leadership (i.e. a portfolio of leadership development opportunities). They might need awareness-based coaching skills and excellent networking skills and be adept at utilizing multiple channels or media to expand knowledge sharing. Leaders must develop an environment and infrastructure which support learning. Communities of (best) practice can facilitate this, underpinned by knowledge-management technology (discussion boards, news groups, LinkedIn group discussions). Physical and virtual space should be branded to reinforce company values for knowledge sharing, opportunities to learn from each other both personally and professionally. Employees learn vicariously through observation of how leaders treat people. The hidden feelings of a culture are the fundamental assumptions and beliefs behind the values and behavioural norms.

Effective interface (trusting relationships)

Fifty per cent of time at work is wasted through lack of trust where people are clearing up issues or dwelling on them rather than being productive. Leaders need to form strong psychological contracts with people; they need excellent communication competence and they must understand how to allow dialogue for the impacts of change to emerge rather than remaining buried. Even the physical space for dialogue and networking in new communities of practice needs to match the values being engendered (e.g. open areas for sharing ideas).

This integrated communications and change approach to managing change also requires all the classic managerial activities of planning, organizing, allocating resources, monitoring and control. In the context of a change programme, these hard management skills remain essential. It produces a degree of predictability and order, and has the potential to consistently produce the short-term results expected by various stakeholders (e.g. for customers, always being on time;

for stockholders, being on budget), but this is simply not the whole gamut of capability making change happen successfully.

LEADERSHIP OF CHANGE VERSUS MANAGEMENT OF CHANGE

The role of the change leader is especially critical and can be defined as: 'Behaving in a way that clearly demonstrates personal commitment and resolve for the people aspects of strategic change at every stage of its implementation.'

Leaders must provide employees with the wherewithal to leave the past behind them and engage with what is to them an unexpected future. A change programme where roles are clearly understood and effectively undertaken is much more likely to succeed and to be sustained into the longer term. Each stakeholder group will be impacted by change in a unique way, their likely emotional range of responses can be envisaged, and your role as a change agent is to work with the information available to mobilize this change and help make it implementable.

Change leadership produces change, often to a dramatic degree, and has the potential to produce extremely useful change (e.g. new products that customers want or new approaches to managing people that make a firm more competitive). However, the expectations can be high at the start of a programme when everything is new but not necessarily understood. As people realize the effect on their own lives, the emotional response can be negative and change leaders need to be able to predict and prepare to deal with this impending reaction (see Figure 8.4).

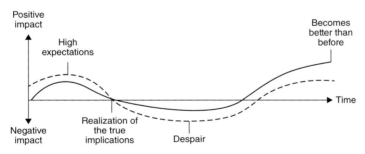

Figure 8.4 An applied Kübler-Ross Change Curve

Change leadership establishes a direction, developing a vision of the future, often the distant future, and strategies needed to achieve that vision. Management activities of planning and budgeting underpin this by establishing detailed project stages, steps and schedules to achieve project goals and (new) business results, and then allocating the resources necessary to make it happen (see Figure 8.5).

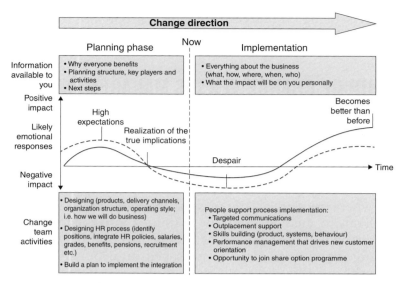

Figure 8.5 Change programme roadmap

Change leadership aligns people whose co-operation may be needed so as to influence the creation of teams and coalitions that understand the vision and strategies and accept their validity. Management activities comprise: organizing and staffing some temporary structure to deliver the planned requirements; hiring suppliers or allocating staff to project team roles; delegating responsibility and authority for carrying out the plan to a PM; providing policies and procedures to help guide people, and creating methods or systems to monitor information.

Change leadership motivates and inspires people to overcome major political, bureaucratic and resource barriers to change by satisfying basic but often unfulfilled human needs. Management activities comprise controlling and problem solving, monitoring results, identifying deviations from plan then planning solutions and organizing to resolve these deviations.

We have seen why PMs need to have a toolbox of influencing strategies to deploy as they discern what is appropriate with each and every different stakeholder or group. This requires each PM to be flexible in their style and adaptable to the demands at different project stages; the degree of directedness or support can be predicted during the planning phases to some extent. By doing your homework on each stakeholder (group and key individual), you will be able to craft relevant messages which will build your credibility in their eyes and their interest in you.

COACH'S TIP

Winning hearts and minds

You must create rapport in your interactions and have emotionally intelligent behaviour in all your communications with stakeholders. It is a cliché to say that you have to plan to win hearts and minds, but neuroscience backs this up with hard evidence of how people communicate deeply with each other in generating trust and achieving agreement. By planning the involvement of stakeholders throughout the project stages, you can create opportunities for monitoring their commitment and consolidate the transition.

Individuals can fulfil more than one role, especially as the change programme progresses. Customers and other influencers will be kept in the loop by means of a communications plan and targeted actions. It is a partnership – with each participant being enrolled and engaged in the content of the change required through excellent communication and influencing skills. Where unions are involved, this may include collective bargaining and building alliances rather than working at the individual level at first. All parties involved in the effective management of change need to:

- recognize that they have a legitimate personal stake in the outcomes
- actively demonstrate personal change and its impact
- be realistic about the benefits to individuals and the emotional costs of change
- engage and enrol others in the leadership team and elsewhere in the organization.

If there are shortfalls in any of these, the change effort will suffer and you may need to consider a more comprehensive leadership development programme.

NEXT STEPS

In this chapter you have been introduced to the concept of change readiness and how it differs from change management. You have carried out an assessment of both your own and your organization's current ability to cope with change, and have used the work of Elisabeth Kübler-Ross to explore how most human beings process significant changes or upheavals by passing through a number of recognizable stages. We looked at an integrated approach to communications and change and have clarified the role and typical responsibilities of change leaders in contrast to managers.

Essentially, this chapter has focused on the change leader's struggle to win over 'hearts' and to nurture the required new mindset, rather than on the mechanics of technical lifecycles which is often portrayed as constituting 'change management'. In the following chapter we will turn the spotlight on the 'touch-feely' stuff – the emotional glue that ensures any project's success.

👍 TAKEAWAYS

What has challenged you the most in reading this chapter and completing the assessments in it?

_____

_____

_____

_____

_____

_____

_____

_____

How do you now see your role as a PM in a change programme?

_____

_____

_____

_____

_____

_____

_____

_____

_____

What will you convey to others about what you have learned from the Kübler-Ross Change Curve, Beckhard's Formula for Change and the Change Wheel explained here?

_____

_____

_____

_____

_____

_____

_____

_____

_____

_____

How would you articulate leadership of change versus management of change?

_____

_____

_____

_____

_____

_____

_____

_____

_____

_____

_____

_____

_____

_____

GENERATING POWERFUL, COLLABORATIVE WORKING RELATIONSHIPS

9

 OUTCOMES FROM THIS CHAPTER

- Understand the importance of powerful and collaborative relationships with stakeholders and colleagues.
- Acquire some relationship tips.
- Understand the role of a sponsor.
- Know how to use your sponsor appropriately.
- Assess the starting basis for your relationship with your sponsor.

Without apology, this chapter is about the touchy-feely stuff – without powerful, collaborative relationships a PM is unlikely to get very far. It is vital to prepare for your first meeting with anyone with power, interest and the potential to back or block the project. For example, the first conversation that you have as a PM with your sponsor needs to be a compelling one; it can be a gateway or a grenade with respect to your part in the outcome of the project. The important relationships could be peer to peer, PM to sponsor, PM to a resource owner, PM to stakeholder group, but they all need to become collaborative, regardless of their initial footing. An outstanding PM creates great relationships with their sponsors.

POWERFUL, COLLABORATIVE WORKING RELATIONSHIPS

When you walk into a meeting room, are you greeted by people whose presence gives you a lift emotionally? Are people pleased to see you? In this workbook, you have already been given a lot of ways of improving your relationships. By progressing through this workbook, you will uncover:

- means of preventing low morale and poor motivation
- influencing skills and strategies to reduce pinch-points and negotiate a smooth path
- proactive measures to avoid or reduce the impact of conflict
- intelligent ways to plan to communicate with stakeholders

- skills to help you become more politically savvy without being a politician
- the importance of powerful and collaborative relationships with stakeholders and colleagues
- methods which can ease the customer journey.

COACH'S TIP

The project glue!

Strong, effective relationships build confidence and trust, acting as the glue holding groups together. Trust underpins project success.

COACHING SESSION 64

Self-assessment: your relationships

Think now about some of your relationships, good and poor. List the characteristics of these people and their relationship with you. Rate their importance on a scale of 1 to 5 where 1 is low. Characteristics are things such as trust, love, safety, agreeing/disagreeing, laughing together, having fun together, admiration, respect, emotional linkage, acceptance, etc. Think of a number of different types of relationship so that you cover a wide spectrum – e.g. partner, non-work friend, work colleague, manager, senior executive. Repeat the exercise for as many relationships as you wish using the following template:

Relationship:	
Characteristic	Importance (1–5)
1	
2	
3	
4	
5	
6	
7	
8	
9	
10	

When you've completed the exercise for all the relationships, identify what makes great relationships, what's lacking in poor relationships and what you could do to make your relationships even better.

Strong, fun relationships

Poor relationships

Make relationships better

What has this coaching session told you about skills and how to improve them?

SOME RELATIONSHIPS TIPS

Here are a few tips to make your everyday relationships go smoothly; often, it's the little things that count:

- **Be outwardly happy.** Enthusiasm is infectious and people will warm to you. Greet people with a cheery 'Hello – how are you?' But don't overplay it. Being overly cheerful for extended periods can become irritating.

- **Show an interest in other people** by getting to know what they like and dislike, their interests and hobbies. If you engage them in 'small talk', avoid gossip around the water cooler; just think about others around you!

- **Don't play office politics.** Take the neutral ground or, even better, challenge the need for political games.

- **Routine office banter can be taken too far** and it's often a short step from banter to bullying or a similar unwarranted behaviour.

- **Organize your time** so that you use it efficiently and delegate appropriately as the PM where you can. That way, you should reduce the amount of time you spend firefighting and have more time for reflection and thinking things through. You'll reduce the pressure on yourself and reward those who seek more responsibility; you'll appear more relaxed and calm. It will rub off on others and positively impact your relationships.

COACHING SESSION 65

Self-assessment: your behaviours

From your own perspective, how regularly do you apply these behaviours at work in your team? Tick the appropriate box for each.

Tip	Never	Rarely	Sometimes	Often	Always
Being outwardly happy					
Showing an interest in others					
Combating office politics					
Watching office banter					
Manage time effectively					
Delegate appropriately					
Add more of your own tips if you wish					

Reflect on your responses regarding relationship tips and describe what you need to do to improve areas of weakness, if any.

_____

_____

_____

_____

THE ROLE OF A SPONSOR

While a PM has to influence all key players in the project, the most important relationship to influence effectively is your sponsor. A project sponsor is an actively engaged senior management role responsible for identifying the business needs and outcomes which take advantage of an opportunity or resolve a problem. The project sponsor (commonly known as the Senior Responsible Owner – SRO) is usually someone with executive authority over the project's budget, scope and scale.

The sponsor needs sufficient power and influence to resolve issues outside of the control of the PM and to maintain the project as a viable business proposition so that the benefits are realized.

The sponsor should help remedy any complicating factors to the smooth running of the project, acting as an intermediary between the project and the organization. The whole language used within the team and within the business may be quite different as a result of your sponsor. The sponsor can act as the 'translator', especially in the early stages, so that the project content and context are aligned. In multinational projects, there may be multiple foreign languages to contend with, not just jargon. Mistranslations and cultural misinterpretation can provoke serious misunderstandings which act like a grenade to relationships.

The PM and sponsor roles require different skills and attributes. The sponsor has the money, the authority and the business need. In hiring a PM, the project sponsor will be looking for someone with drive, energy, experience, knowledge and intelligence (both intellectual and emotional).

If the sponsor has hired the PM, then the PM usually hires the project team with agreed delegated limits of funding, in the hope that this will engender a sense of loyalty throughout the chain of command.

USING YOUR SPONSOR APPROPRIATELY

Developing greater perception, shrewdness and subtle influence in the workplace by deploying better political savvy can reduce stress at work for you and your team. Generating a powerful working relationship with your sponsors involves as a starting basis a significant number of variable factors which are hard to predict. Your sponsor may have been automatically appointed by an executive because they do not see the role as sufficiently important for them to take it on or because it involves subjects in which they do not have a great deal of expertise or experience. A PM needs to understand the organization in order to help them ensure that they have been assigned the most appropriate, powerful sponsors.

 COACH'S TIP

Finding the right sponsor

It is possible to change the sponsor in the early project stages, as there are usually governance meetings with other potential champions. But it is essential to understand how to select the project sponsors that will add the maximum value to a project. These days, in most cases IT runs your business, yet it took quite some time before the head person in IT got a board position as opposed to reporting to the chief operating officer (COO).

The sponsor must take their role seriously and be honest about their day job and what has to be delegated, so that they can devote quality time to the project sponsor role. The PM may find they can augment the motivation of the sponsor. Gaining understanding of what the role demands is essential and being able to communicate the value to a prospective or current sponsor in an engaging way is vital. The use of a responsibility assignment matrix to reduce team confrontations and clarify other key parties' responsibilities is essential.

In addition to the management basics of business cases, vision documents, schedules and plan, check that your sponsor supports your responsibilities by:

- creating a climate at work and environment in which the project can succeed
- ensuring consistency of project management methods and techniques
- aiding resource finding, allocation and firm commitment
- aiding the resolution of conflicts
- sounding out ideas, providing proactive and helpful 'checks and balances'.

Equally, a PM needs to appreciate what a sponsor may reasonably expect from them. This may come through in the first meeting. However, two-way expectations must be articulated and not left unsaid:

- Any hidden agenda on the part of the sponsor may be unpicked by an astute PM as the project goes on. But do you know enough about your sponsor? Have you got their trust, or is there something non-verbal that hints at a lack of trust? What are you hearing or seeing that indicates that you need to identify subplots and hidden agendas. A political agenda is one which may put a personal slant on an established change agenda and agreed purpose of a project; a person may give the agreed change project purpose a spin to more closely match their needs or the aspirations of a group of allied stakeholders. If you have any experience of the politics turning on you, then you are wise to build a strong relationship with your sponsor. Find out what they need from you and learn from their experience.

- You should also have a good idea what your sponsor knows about you. This chapter helps you to know what you are aiming for. You must start the relationship on a straight footing. You must use what is under your nose: trust, respect and rapport.

- What are the key interdependencies within the relationship between the PM role and the sponsor? Are they healthy interdependencies such as the sharing of ideas? What are the co-dependencies? These are the unhealthy factors such as where the PM may be playing 'the sacrificial lamb' or where the PM may be making the relationship with the sponsor more important than it is. What is the collateral damage on communication and key relationships because of these co-dependencies? The PM and sponsor need to joined at the hip on the end-to-end communications strategy. Will they fund specialist communications help, and, if so, do they understand modern channels and social media?

- In matrix management situations, PMs are given their resources by an immediate superior or line manager for an agreed period of time. If relationships between you and a line manager are not strong enough to secure a firm commitment, use your sponsor to secure resource agreements.

- How long will the sponsor be around – will they see the whole lifespan of the project through and be responsible for delivering the benefits?

By completing all of the coaching sessions in the chapters up to this one, the management information that you should now have available to you will be immense. By completing a thorough map of stakeholders, relationships and the organizational landscape, an astute PM can identify whether their sponsor is straightforward or playing some sort of game with others in power who have an interest in and influence over the project.

Both the sponsor and the PM need to more than pay for themselves by bringing the project in on time, to budget and to quality expectations – good ones always do so. If your sponsor is not sufficiently powerful and influential, you need to act early on to get the authority commensurate with the demands of your role and the intended business outcome. It is tricky to have to act once weak sponsorship is apparent, but such a serious risk must be mitigated.

The early governance meetings (to approve the business case and project strategy) are an opportunity for powerful, active and supportive stakeholders to be identified. The key thing here is to have completed all of the stakeholder coaching sessions in the preceding chapters and to have done your homework with subtlety when preparing your approach:

- Review the management information that you have collected by doing the coaching sessions. Evaluate how this is relevant to the sponsor/PM relationship.

- In analysing and assessing stakeholders, filters should have been applied which prioritize those who need to be kept informed, and which identify how this leaves you and your sponsor in terms of allies and positive help with which to work.

- Assess how astute, well informed and good a champion the sponsor and other project board members are. What influence and relevant connections have they got?

⏼⏼ COACHING SESSION 66

Your organization and workplace politics

The results of a survey conducted by the British Computer Society Chartered Institute for Information Technology highlighted some interesting points which can be used to help a PM understand the political behaviour which causes conflict in project relationships:

- 45% of senior managers admitted being likely to engage in workplace politics and are thus the group most likely to do so. 37% of other staff admitted to personally engaging in political behaviour.

- Only 14% of technical staff would engage in political behaviour and are therefore the least likely to do so among all staff groups.

- 59% of people reported that having different goals or agendas caused conflict.

- 51% of people reported that having power or status issues caused conflict.

- 51% reported that differences over ways of doing things caused conflict.

- 55% believe that political behaviour has increased within their organization in recent years.

- Surprisingly, 57% reported that they avoided politics or pretended that political behaviour did not exist at all; their preferred method of dealing with conflict was inaction.

How do the above survey results correlate to your circumstances?

COACHING SESSION 67

Assessment: your sponsor and you

In this coaching session you are asked to reflect on a number of questions which may seem uncomfortable to contemplate. The answers will help you to identify who and what you require to achieve the requisite power, influence and backing to succeed in your project's mission and PM role.

Question	Answer
Who sponsors your project and how do they feel about their role?	
What is the sponsor's belief about how people are motivated?	
What support will they give if 'hygiene factors' are an issue?	
How well balanced are the responsive and assertive skills of the sponsor (are they all push or all pull, or somewhere in between)?	
Is there anything you need to manage in terms of a lack of finesse on their part? Can you help them?	
Is the sponsor personal friends with influential or powerful people and is this an influencing strategy?	

Question	Answer
INFLUENCING STRATEGIES – what does this sponsor see as their role in building alliances, bargaining, visioning/inspiration, empowerment, use of position power, expertise and information access?	
How are they rated by their peers for the sponsor role? Does the sponsor have any history with other authority figures you need to know about?	
How do they feel about your appointment to the PM role?	
Regarding winning more collaboration and avoiding conflict, who does what and how? Contextualize this in terms of what tools you have in your armoury?	
Is there any push-back from the sponsor on how you want to build your team? Good PMs would not need to defer to the sponsor or other line managers.	
Who owns the skilled resources for each project stage? Refer to the lifecycle exercise (Coaching session 44) in Chapter 5 as required.	
What would be the outcome of talking things over with your sponsor to get their expertise, experience and insight on how to avoid conflict proactively?	
Who else needs those resources at the same time or during an adjacent time period? Identify cross-project dependencies.	

Question	Answer
How will slippage affect resource allocation? Will they be removed from your resource list and allocated to another PM on a given date, thereby leaving a resource gap?	
What alternative ways of filling the resource gap are there and at what cost? Identify advantages and disadvantages.	
What alternative project strategy, technical lifecycle or procurement options are there if you are unable to fill this resource gap?	

Having considered the above, what changes do you need to make happen in order to get the backing the project needs and to achieve the power and influence required to succeed in your role?

_____

_____

_____

_____

_____

_____

_____

_____

_____

→ NEXT STEPS

This chapter encouraged you to think carefully about your relationship with your sponsor and other powerful, collaborative relationships. The next two chapters look at some contextual hiccups which can occur where the standards being applied remain unchallenged. For example, many of us experience programme management which does not handle the customer's journey very well.

TAKEAWAYS

What one new thing will you do to make you much more successful in terms of relationships?

_____

_____

_____

_____

_____

_____

_____

_____

_____

_____

What are the most important things that you can do for your sponsor?

_____

_____

_____

_____

_____

_____

_____

_____

_____

_____

_____

_____

What are the most important things that your sponsor can do for you and your project?

_____

_____

_____

_____

_____

_____

_____

_____

_____

_____

What parameters did you use to prioritize stakeholders?

_____

_____

_____

_____

_____

_____

_____

_____

_____

_____

_____

HELPING THE CUSTOMER JOURNEY

10

 OUTCOMES FROM THIS CHAPTER

- Identify the right questions to ask.
- Know how to get the right level and type of support.
- Define the requirements with customers.
- Use a creative problem-solving process.
- Consider what else we can do to ease the customer journey through a project.

The premise that we can predict things to any great degree is wrong. However, the means to work collaboratively in order to muster more power to analyse big questions is improving exponentially. There is a belief in the business world that is false: 'We are rational autonomous beings.' We use experience (or perceptions from our senses) to ground beliefs which we have about things that we have not observed. Change agents need to be realistic about what we can hope will happen after we have left. All we *can* do is the *best* we can do while we are there, putting in place the best workable practice. In this chapter you will find a few ideas to help the project definition and customer journey to ease clarity, thus avoiding confusion.

ASKING THE RIGHT QUESTIONS

How do you currently provide the answers to the following questions?

- Are we making the right investments?
- Are we continuing with the best-value programmes and projects?
- Are we serving our stakeholders in the right way?
- How much money will we spend collectively and for what return?
- What programmes and projects under our control are delivering the best value?
- What resources are available to us and what are our options?
- If we have to alter priorities immediately, because of policy or strategy changes, where can we get funding out of our existing portfolio?

- Which programmes and projects should we stop, and what are the consequences?
- Are we making the best use of our resources, spending our finances correctly and making the right decisions based on the facts?
- Can we respond effectively to external information requests quickly, efficiently and factually?

GETTING THE RIGHT LEVEL AND TYPE OF SUPPORT

If your organization is unable to answer these questions, it probably does not have the right level of support. The customer for the project needs to have fact-based evidence of the status of a project. Having this evidence considerably eases their engagement and buy-in to investing in a project's product or outcome.

It very much eases the customer journey if your organization is running an investment strategy to set up specialist support. It is best practice to:

- manage business value in investments
- manage risks in the business, the investment portfolio and its programmes and projects
- have skilled resources that help change managers at all three levels: portfolio, programme and project (P3O).

The P3O supports decision-making by providing fact-based evidence for those decisions. P3O staff also helps change managers at each level with delivery according to the requirements and service levels agreed. You may need to carry out a survey of customers' perceptions of support.

Example questions examining what customers think of a P3O's services are given in the following template, which is downloadable from www.consultationltd. com/PMCoach.

Question	Customer perception
1 Is there a documented P3O vision?	
2 Are there clear terms of reference (TOR) for each part of the P3O?	
3 Are these TOR fully understood by the relevant P3O staff members?	
4 Do the stakeholders agree that the TOR are being met?	
5 Does the organization require P3O support for projects and programmes using specialist skills in any of the following areas?	

Question	Customer perception
• workshop facilitation	
• planning	
• risk and issue management	
• procurement	
• supplier management	
• quality assurance	
• financial control	
• application of project/programme standards and methods	
• benefits management	
• configuration management	
• change control	
• communications and stakeholder engagement	
6 For each area of expertise: If so, are the requirements adequately satisfied? If not, where are the shortfalls?	
7 What value does each level of the P3O add to the organization?	

Portfolio

- Is it a respected information hub?

- Does it provide the right level of information to support decision-making by senior management?

- Does it reassure senior management that they are optimizing their investment in change?

Programme

- Does it support programme and project management effectively?

- Does it ensure the viability of outcomes?

- Does it support the relevant projects effectively?

- Does it assist the PM in delivering to the required tolerances of time, cost and quality?

- Do the relevant parts of the P3O support reviews of projects and programmes?

- If so, does the P3O involvement enable swift and effective review processes wherever they are needed?

COACHING SESSION 68

Assessment: information management

1. Are all levels collecting, collating and analysing information from the same data sources? Or are different processes duplicating the keying in of information from feeder systems (i.e. requiring re-entry of similar or identical information in different forms)?

2. How does your organization manage business value versus technical risks?

3. How does your project get its funding and how are changing priorities managed?

4. How do you decide what is right for your organization and its investment?

DEFINING REQUIREMENTS

The biggest issue in IT projects is the uncertainty at the beginning of the project about what customers actually need. The modern rate of technological development means that the mainstream customer may not be sufficiently savvy to inspire your development team through a statement of needs. Enthusiasts of 'lean' and 'agile' methods would argue that that uncertainty is why such methods cater for it – traditional predictive methods simply do not deal with ambiguity. This is dealt with in Chapter 11.

However, if you are following a more linear lifecycle, you may run events with customers to help them discover and define their needs. You and your business analysts may have good facilitation skills (plus user experience staff, technical writers and so on) to work with customers on achieving clarity. The following mnemonic can be used to reduce ambiguity and structure user requirements – FLURPIS.

Requirement	Operational requirement
Functionality	Describes each of the functional requirements of the system. Each function description should be no more than a couple of sentences. Complex functions should be broken down into simpler functions. Remember, all communities' needs should be considered such as auditors' access and auditing requirements.
Localization	Are there any complicating factors such as national security constraints, culture, foreign language, dialect and technical jargon which make this business product less generic and more unique or specific? Are there terminology or industry compliance constraints? Consider things concerned with the site geography such as remote working from home, disability requirements and a need for mobile connectivity for travelling personnel.
Usability	What mechanisms, software structures or techniques will enhance the ease of use of the system? Are there any user preferences for ergonomic design?
Reliability	What are the business needs for reliability which may justify additional cost, service levels, technologies and/or equipment (e.g. recoverability of data)?
Performance	Can any parameters and metrics be given regarding tangible aspects of user requirements, such as response time, system availability, through-put and other capacity measures?
Integration	Specify the systems that the requirements solution will have to interface with and the compatibility factors which have to be taken into account – e.g. use of Windows, security required, etc.
Supportability	What are the non-functional requirements of the system that mean it can be kept secure and working reliably and robustly? Include access permissions such as physical security, passwords, standby processing arrangements or business continuity planning plus data and system backup. How easy can this system be made to maintain and support? What will the cost of ownership be like? What knock-on effect is there on other business systems and processes?

COACHING SESSION 69

Create a FLURPIS table

Create a table using the FLURPIS mnemonic to describe your own project.

Requirement	Your requirement
Functionality	
Localization	
Usability	
Reliability	
Performance	
Integration	
Supportability	

COACH'S TIP

Improve the customer journey

Use FLURPIS in combination with a creative thinking process such as the one described in Chapter 1 and the one below to help move the customer journey from uncertainty to a greater level of definition of needs and priorities.

A CREATIVE PROBLEM-SOLVING TECHNIQUE

This is a brainstorming technique that relies on you being able to define a good question to put though the ideas generation process (Figure 10.1).

The natural flip-flopping of the brain between divergent and convergent thinking can be channelled by following the steps described. You need to focus and be calm mentally to do this and stick with the process during the early learning phases with no distractions. It requires discipline, but it is well worth it.

Each style of thinking has several stages and steps. This creative problem-solving process uses divergence followed by convergence, which mirrors the natural habit of the brain to expand ideas and then to filter, sift, prioritize and sort ideas. The discipline is in maintaining divergent thinking, which generates ideas and insights for as long as feasible, before allowing the evaluation of each idea. You must suspend convergent thinking because this shuts down idea generation and focuses on critiques of what has been produced.

Figure 10.1 Facilitation skills: You need confident and flexible facilitation skills as well as the ability to carry this process off; otherwise your customers will get lost in the process.

- **Ground rules for divergence**
    - Defer your judgement of other people's ideas including your own.
    - Strive for quantity: there's nothing more dangerous than an idea when it's the only one you've got!
    - Seek wild and unusual ideas: it's easier to tame a wild idea than invigorate a weak one.
    - Build on other ideas: piggybacking on ideas is creative.
- **Ground rules for convergence**
    - Use affirmative judgement: focus on the benefits and potential before looking at obstacles.
    - Be deliberate: don't let your emotions distort your thinking.
    - Check objectives: keep on target.
    - Combine ideas: to create stronger solutions.
    - Consider novelty: give even the strangest ideas a chance.

Do not try to remember the process all at once; step through it using the following pages as crib sheets. With practice, you will gradually learn the technique and the benefits of using it. The first thing is to carefully describe the nature of the problem that you would like an answer to and shape it as a question.

Identify a question that you would like the answer to or formulate a description of a problem that you want the solution to.

 COACH'S TIP

Questions, questions…

For examples of questions, look back at the investment and portfolio office support section earlier in this chapter – for example:

- Are we making the right investments?
- How do we know whether the programmes and projects are right for us?

The **three main steps** are:

1. Frame the problem to understand the challenge.

2. Generate ideas (use divergent thinking to come up with ideas and not immediately evaluate ideas).

3. Select and strengthen solutions and prepare for action.

Step 1: frame the problem to understand the challenge

Let's take as our question 'How do we know whether the programmes and projects are right for us?' List all of the associated things you need to solve to answer this question. Look at the question and think: 'What else arises that we need to solve?'

Preparing to be more creative involves letting go:

- Open your mind.

- Drop all assumptions.

- Defer your judgement.

- Be interested in everything.

- See things like a child.

- Why is it a problem?

- What's stopping us?

- In what way might we do this?

Then review/overview:

- Ask both yourself and the group 'What else?' For example, you might ask how to prioritize conflicting demands for resources and investment to leverage greater revenues from existing accounts.

- Refine the question or specific problem statement so that it loses any ambiguity. Try experimenting by changing the language or broadening the problem (e.g. from financial management to asset management).

- Next go wild and wacky to create the most extraordinary associations which can later be brought back into the problem statement (remember Coaching session 3, which asked you to describe your car).

Step 2: generate ideas

Describe solutions by generating ideas about the value they add, their potential, things to watch for and reasons to make them happen, recording them on flipcharts as follows:

Positive	Potential	Concerns	Outcome and opportunity
Value added by the solution	What's the potential?	What to watch for	Why we'd want to do it
e.g. Manage sensitively as part of normal process	e.g. Consensus and ability to plan	e.g. Polarized positions	e.g. Be more productive with less management overhead
Tip: Use the mnemonic FLURPIS above	*Tip:* Not too short and not too long	*Hint:* Create as rich a picture as possible	*Tip:* Be innovative and comprehensive

Create your own version of the table for your project to complete.

Step 3: select and strengthen solutions and prepare for action

Select and strengthen the solutions – can you add more value to the solution somehow? Are there identified concerns and risks that you can provide mitigation for? Can you increase the incentives of why it should be done (better, faster, cheaper)? Prepare for action – think about the skilled resources and funding, facilities and their likely availability for action. Use your project planning skills to scope it out and level out the resource requirements, sequencing and priorities.

Wrapping it up

Remember that the premise for carrying out process such as the technique above is that the customer needs help in defining their requirements unambiguously. Also, consider the emotional capital of the experience of doing this creative problem-solving exercise by asking the following questions:

- **Self-awareness** What am I feeling now?
- **Self-control** What can I do about it?
- **Social-awareness** What are the other group members feeling?
- **Relationship management** How do I want us to feel at the end? What emotions do I want us to feel at the end of this process?

Check understanding by encouraging customers to articulate their understanding and feelings at the end of the process.

COACHING SESSION 70

What application of the FLURPIS technique and the creative problem-solving process can you use to practise getting clarity and helping the customer journey?

_____

_____

_____

_____

_____

_____

_____

OTHER GOOD PRACTICES

Other good practices to help the customer get clarity in defining requirements are more methodology-dependent, for example:

- **Use cases making viable options** The use case model captures the requirements of a system. Use cases are a means of communicating what the system is intended to do to users and other stakeholders. It is useful to have a usability definition and set business rules for developers to create great usability.

- **Target operating model** This describes, for example, the future state in terms of the people, culture, values, business rules, value proposition, processes, behaviours, technology, products, customers (journeys, segmentation, touch point for each journey), market, territories, financial performance forecasts, partners, business ethics, volumetric data, supply chain, estates/sites and logistics.

- **Vision document** This covers the vision, value proposition, usage scenario, 'know your users', users' language, most common tasks, main processes, navigation, mock-ups and non-functional requirements – they are always needed, so don't forget them.

COACHING SESSION 71

Which of the above can you use in order to practise achieving clarity and helping the customer journey?

_____

_____

_____

_____

_____

_____

_____

_____

_____

_____

_____

_____

_____

_____

_____

_____

_____

_____

→ NEXT STEPS

In this chapter we focused on asking the right questions to check that you are making the right investment in change; getting the right level and type of support at portfolio, programme and project levels; defining requirements with customers using techniques which deal with the uncertainty and ambiguity of their understanding of their requirements in the early stages, and using a creative problem-solving process to brainstorm ideas.

The next chapter, on 'lean' and 'agile' approaches, is most certainly relevant to helping the customer journey to be more productive (better, faster and cheaper).

👍 TAKEAWAYS

How does your project fit into the investment portfolio of the organization?

_____

_____

_____

_____

_____

_____

_____

_____

How do you manage risks in the business, the investment portfolio and its programmes and projects?

_____

_____

_____

_____

_____

_____

_____

_____

_____

_____

As a result of customer feedback on using the exercises with them, what could be improved about your method of eliciting customer requirements?

_____

_____

_____

_____

_____

_____

_____

_____

_____

Use one of the other good practices and reflect on the utility of its application in your organization.

_____

_____

_____

_____

_____

_____

_____

_____

_____

_____

_____

'LEAN' AND 'AGILE' APPROACHES

11

 OUTCOMES FROM THIS CHAPTER

- Contrast and compare traditional and 'agile' development methods.
- Consider the principles and tools of a 'lean' approach and what this might mean for your organization.

In the last 15 years there has been a rise in systems development lifecycles which reject traditional 'waterfall' models because the latter do not cater for the rapid product development capability needed owing to global market forces. Much of what stakeholders need can be delivered if the culture has a 'lean' and 'agile' mindset on how the organization is run; this state of mind and attitude to change greases the wheels of transformation. The former total quality management approach to lean manufacturing and transforming business operations has morphed into lean methods and other philosophies for quality management, the elimination of waste and continuous improvement.

TRADITIONAL DEVELOPMENT METHODS

Methods exist on a continuum from 'adaptive' to 'predictive', with agile methods on the adaptive side. Adaptive methods focus on adapting quickly to changing realities; when the needs of a project or business change, an adaptive team changes as well.

Predictive methods, in contrast, focus on analysing and planning the future in detail and catering for known risks. In the extremes, a predictive team can report exactly what features and tasks are planned for the entire length of the development process; an agile team can report what the next sprint or scrum cycle might contain subject to change described later in this chapter. A traditional product delivery lifecycle (PDL) is composed of a series of predictive stages, as in Figure 11.1:

Traditionally, predictive methods of this type have the following characteristics:

- Early phase analysis, fixing the requirements specification, and thus having difficulty subsequently changing direction.

- A change control board to lock down the requirements specification at the start and test the whole system against requirements at the end.

- Governance with gateways authorizing the next step and approving the outputs of the previous one by a project board and/or a steering committee.

- Stringent controls over budget, procurement, supplier payments and benefits management with even quite small sums needing senior management sign-off.

- An audit trail of sign-offs by different teams, brand, compliance procedures, legal (e.g. Sarbanes Oxley design and delivery compliance, cookies, competition law) and audit.

- Mandatory deliverables with minimum content requirements (usually).

- Six-month incremental phased development to enable stakeholders to see a release of an enhanced product which in reality takes up to 18 months to complete.

Figure 11.1 Product development lifecycle

Traditional governance hierarchies have roles and relationships as illustrated in Figure 11.2.

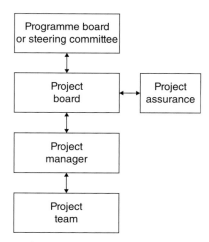

Figure 11.2 Traditional governance hierarchy

AGILE METHODS

An agile organization contrasts strongly with this governance model. An alternative is agile software development, which is based on iterative and incremental development where requirements and solutions evolve through collaboration between self-organizing, cross-functional teams. In 2001, 17 software developers met to discuss lightweight development methods. The result was the *Agile Manifesto*.

 ONLINE RESOURCE

The Agile Manifesto

Download the *Agile Manifesto* to gain an illuminating insight into the agile method and philosophy.

www.TYCoachbooks.com/ProjectManagement

An agile software development approach can be described as follows:

- It is a conceptual framework that promotes foreseen interactions throughout the development cycle. Agile development delivers a shippable new product or increment of business value in a fast time at an acceptable price.

- It is a time-boxed iterative approach made up of 'Sprints' (usually a month of coding or less), which encourages rapid and flexible response to change.

- The agile approach builds a set of options rather than a single solution early in the lifecycle and this manages the innate uncertainty which exists in IT projects. Thus, crucial decisions are delayed until customers have better evaluated their needs.

- A Sprint is a known amount of resource in an agreed timeframe developing a product increment with known business value (features, business processes and changes of items on the product backlog).

- Sprint planning activities are concentrated on alternative options and adapt to the current situation. Planning discussions can clarify confusing situations by establishing patterns for rapid action (thus mistaken design assumptions and other errors are avoided or reduced).

Evolutionary development will balance highest business value items with highest technical risk, and preparation for the first Sprint Cycle involves the following (Figure 11.3):

- joint diagnosis, vision and strategy, business case and funding
- contractual agreement
- initial product backlog
- initial release plan
- stakeholder buy-in
- assembly of the Scrum Team energized through daily Scrum stand-up meetings to produce a product increment.

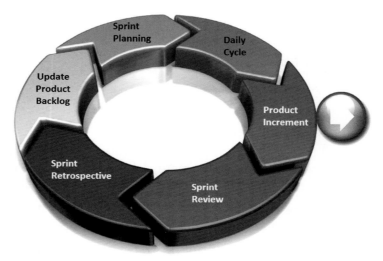

Figure 11.3 The Sprint Cycle

Sprint Planning

A company has to predict peaks and troughs of Sprint resources so the supplier or HR can roll resources off the client site and back on for major demands. Thus, delayed decisions caused, say, by a waterfall lifecycle amalgamated with the Scrum process are expensive.

The value to the customer of the pilot product option or shipped increment may be the same as what they paid for it or it may be of greater value – the difference is a piece of consumer feedback worth the Product Manager knowing. The building of options earlier in the lifecycle allows for adaptation to change and the prevention of costly technology-bounded decisions. Agile software uses a different mindset and organizational structure in comparison to traditional methods.

Unlike a waterfall model process, an agile team will have difficulty describing exactly what will happen in the future and cannot report exactly what tasks they will complete next month, but the Scrum Master can report which features they plan for the next Sprint Cycle. When asked about a release six months from now, an agile team might explain the mission statement of expected value versus cost and they may employ highly disciplined formal methods for quality assurance.

The Product Owner (with advice from technical writers, programmers and quality-assurance staff) steers the Sprint Planning meeting using the Product Backlog to identify which items to work on first and the first Sprint Cycle might develop the whole system in skeleton form. The original creative concept is developed by the Product Owner and his/her user experience specialists. Evaluating different options is effective as soon as it is realized that they are not free of charge, but they provide the necessary flexibility for later decision-making.

While major decisions are left as late as feasible to allow users' understanding of their needs to mature, the Product Owner steers the Sprint content to maintain visibility of the business value. However, the Sprint Cycle and Daily Scrum process may be delegated to a change manager to oversee production of the functionality expected to be delivered.

The Scrum Team will break down the chosen items into tasks which can be estimated in size to fill a Sprint Cycle. The Product Owner will add items to the Sprint until its capacity is fully utilized. The Sprint's composition is a balance of technical risk against delivered business value (better, faster, cheaper). An item is not complete until it is coded, tested and documented. Typically, the trained Scrum Team is orchestrated by the Scrum Master for the Product Owner and is composed as shown in Figure 11.4.

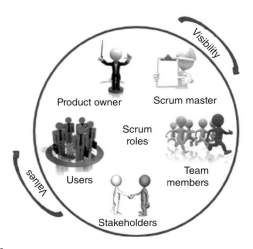

Figure 11.4 The Scrum Team

Daily Cycle

Daily Scrum meetings are a lean approach to pulling all necessary actions together without any wasted activity. Everyone stands up to induce shorter discussions of about 15 minutes and each person answers three questions:

- What did you do?

- What will you do today?

- What impediments do you have?

If it becomes evident that two or more people need to share with each other for longer, the Scrum Master defines the needed conversation which ensures that the expected output is made clear and the time agreed (usually that day / as soon as possible).

COMPARISON OF TRADITIONAL AND AGILE DEVELOPMENT METHODS

Differences between agile and traditional methods such as waterfall are:

- Testing of the software is conducted at different points during the software development lifecycle.

- In the waterfall model, there is a separate testing phase near the point of implementation.

- In the agile development method decisions may be made as late as possible to allow the business drivers' and stakeholders' product conceptualization to mature as much as feasible in an acceptable timeframe.

- Situation-appropriateness can be considered a distinguishing characteristic between agile and traditional methods, with the latter being more rigid and prescriptive. Agile methods allow project teams to adapt working practices according to the needs of individual projects. (Practices are concrete activities and products that are part of a method framework.)

- Agile methods work to engage customers and end-users to facilitate business agility where testing is done concurrently with implementation.

Systems development lifecycles and lean and agile capability are still not as mature or pervasive as they have the potential to be. The field lacks clarity, which is unsurprising perhaps, given that agile methods insist on 'working software over documentation' and welcoming change rather than rigid process. In the last decade:

- Agile has moved from being an idea on the fringe of software development to something approaching the mainstream

- Differing methodologies have proliferated, ideas have matured, and many more organizations have adopted agile though not always successfully

- The traditional lifecycle has been combined with a Sprint Cycle in recent years; but this arrangement may not prove defensible. Economically successful examples of amalgamated methods are not yet proven.

Using an agile approach for a 'big bang' programme is not a credible option; not so long ago a UK government department announced the world's biggest agile development programme. Yet a two-year gap between incremental deliveries of modules has since arisen. This high-profile UK public-sector project has written off £34 million (announced in September 2013) and apparently cannot guarantee good value on the £303 million already expended out of a total budget of £2.4 billion. The auditors observed that 'they experienced problems incorporating the agile approach into existing contracts, governance and assurance structures'.

One expert commented that 'the procurement decisions appear to have been taken before agile was even thought of as a delivery approach and appear to be at odds with agile delivery'. I do not believe that 'big bang' development is what agile software development was created to do; calling a project 'agile' does not make it agile.

One of the business risks with adoption is a cultural one around documentation; agile people are reluctant to believe it is something they need to do. Enthusiasts argue that the product will be around for so little time that they ask why documentation is useful.

- The year 2000 'Millennium Bug' demonstrated that systems last more than five years (code was being changed that dated from the 1980s), so documentation is necessary even if it is written after it has been coded and tested, because programmers leave organizations frequently.

- Business processes are part of the business value and must be shareable.

- Modern agile development tools probably have automated documentation tools, too, to aid completion.

Many businesses use agile development methods with an outsourced supply chain. Theoretically, outsourcing is viewed as cheaper than employing permanent employees in the company.

- However, what are the costs of the management overhead and the measurement of quality of delivery?

- What are the knock-on effects of added complexities such as:
  - technical staff speaking English as a foreign language
  - challenges to businesspeople understanding technical jargon with a foreign accent
  - outsourcing colocation issues, time zones and geography.

In my experience, getting business value, quality and a low management overhead easily out of this type of contract is a challenge too far.

The benefits of delivering 'early and often' can be financial, marketing or engineering (and others). The fundamental rationale behind why delivering 'early and often' helps increase value is by improving the financial case, driving faster feedback to lessen risk, and provides flexibility to improve the flow of work.

COACHING SESSION 72

Becoming agile

Explore the three dimensions of 'better', 'cheaper' and 'faster' where you can pick any two but it is not possible to optimize all three; one dimension will always suffer. Here 'faster' refers to the time required to deliver the product, 'better' is the quality of the final product, and 'cheaper' refers to the total cost of designing and building the product. For example:

- Design something quickly to a high standard and it will not be cheap.
- Design something quickly and cheaply and it will not be of high quality.
- Design something with high quality and cheaply, but it will not be quick.

1. Reflect on your current project and make any analogies with previous projects – what balance was achieved on each of them?

_____

_____

_____

_____

_____

2. How do you rate your current level of agility as an organization?

_____

_____

_____

_____

_____

3. What does an agile organization look like to you?

_____

_____

_____

_____

_____

_____

4. How would you rate your current change readiness and maturity?

_____

_____

_____

_____

_____

5. What are the implications for your organization of your current ability to become more 'lean' and 'agile'?

_____

_____

_____

_____

_____

6. What actions do you plan to take as a result of your thinking in answering the above questions?

_____

_____

_____

7. What is your organization's process for questioning all existing techniques and systems by asking *where* the organization should stand in the marketplace, and *how* to be creative and innovative to succeed in the marketplace?

8. Define the benefits of delivering early and often: financial, marketing, engineering and other.

The constraints of project management used to be visualized as a 'time, cost and quality' triangle. However, nowadays this has been adapted, so that quality is in the centre of the triangle with scope, cost and schedule as the points.

9. What are the flaws in focusing solely on the triangle of time, cost and quality?

_____

_____

10. What are the common problems and the unintended consequences of traditional project management and development methods?

_____

_____

_____

_____

_____

_____

How can your organization change in order to deliver software and IT better? Do people understand and recognize the scale of issues in existing software development and delivery?

11. What is the imperative for changing the way you develop software now?

_____

_____

_____

_____

_____

12. What are the better ways of working and why do you expect people to find change so hard and resist alternative methods of working?

_____

_____

_____

_____

_____

_____

_____

13. Identify how software development can be made more intuitive through faster feedback.

_____

_____

_____

_____

_____

_____

Develop an action plan as you work through your answers to the above questions. Develop your own list but also get feedback on the things that you need to start doing, stop doing, do more of or do less of.

Action plan	
I will start...	I will do more...
I will stop...	I will do less of...

THE PRINCIPLES OF A LEAN MINDSET

'A [lean] mindset, or way of thinking, [is] a commitment to achieve a totally waste-free operation that's focused on your customer's success... It is achieved by simplifying and continuously improving all processes and relationships in an environment of trust, respect and full employee involvement... It is about people, simplicity, flow, visibility, partnerships and true value as perceived by the customer.'

David Hogg, High Performance Solutions

Lean Thinking is about the elimination of waste in any part of a business – for example, taking a raw material through to a fully shippable product with steps that add value at each point and do so with no nugatory activities. Mary Poppendieck describes an approach to lean thinking, as follows:

'**Start with an inspiring purpose**, and overcome the curse of short-term thinking.

Energise teams by providing well-framed challenges, larger purposes, and a direct line of sight between their work and the achievement of those purposes.

Delight customers by gaining unprecedented insight into their real needs, and building products and services that fully anticipate those needs.

Achieve authentic, sustainable efficiency without layoffs, rock-bottom cost focus, or totalitarian work systems.

Develop breakthrough innovations by moving beyond predictability to experimentation, beyond globalisation to decentralisation, beyond productivity to impact.'

The Seven Wastes

Regardless of sector, private, public or voluntary, the elimination of waste focuses on removing nugatory activity in processes. WORMPIT is a mnemonic for 'Waiting, Overproduction, Repair, Motion, Over-processing, Inventory and Transportation' (see Figure 11.5). All steps should contain activities that add value, so they are honed down to the least possible work adding the maximum amount of value. These lean processes can be tailored to industry, commerce or functions such as IT.

Figure 11.5 WORMPIT

Types of waste in lean IT

Lean Thinking takes a little effort to transfer out of its roots in manufacturing and into IT transactions, but it is worth the learning curve. Lean principles applied to IT replaces 'raw material being transformed into a product' with 'data being turned into information, know-how and intellectual property' which has business value.

Lean IT is the extension of lean manufacturing and lean services principles applied to the development and management of IT products and services. Each element in the table below could be a significant source of waste in itself, but a greater cascade of waste can result from the linkages between elements (often called 'the domino effect').

Waste element	Examples	Business outcome
Defects	• Unauthorized system and application changes • Substandard project execution	Poor customer service, increased costs
Overproduction (Overprovisioning)	• Unnecessary delivery of low-value applications and services	Business and IT misalignment; increased costs and overheads: energy, data centre space, maintenance
Waiting	• Slow application response times • Manual service escalation procedures	Lost revenue, poor customer service, and reduced productivity

Waste element	Examples	Business outcome
Non-value-added processing	• Reporting technology metrics to business managers	Miscommunication
Transportation	• On-site visits to resolve hardware and software issues • Physical software, security and compliance audits	Higher capital and operational expenses
Inventory (excess)	• Server sprawl, under-utilized hardware • Multiple repositories to handle risks and control • Benched application development teams	Increased costs: data centre, energy; lost productivity
Motion (excess)	• Firefighting repeat problems within the IT infrastructure and applications	Lost productivity
Employee knowledge (unused)	• Failing to capture ideas/innovation • Knowledge and experience retention issues • Employees spend time on repetitive or mundane tasks	Talent leakage, low job satisfaction, increased support and maintenance costs

Source: http://en.wikipedia.org/wiki/Lean_IT

For example, if there are faults in your ecommerce (merchandized) website which make it very unresponsive when a customer is trying to browse products and complete a transaction to buy, they may abandon their shopping basket and either call the customer centre or phone a local retail store:

■ The retail store may have face-to-face customers who need staff attention rather than dealing with the phone call from an online customer.

■ The customer centre may get overloaded with calls because of the slow website.

■ The ecommerce site may have many abandoned online shopping baskets that have to be dealt with by ecommerce staff or user-experience managers investigating performance and identifying the problem coincidentally.

■ The company may also introduce additional server capacity to speed the response time and hire extra customer support agents to compensate for some technical defect that needs repair.

■ There is no added value in the customer transactions – it is all costing money and therefore contributes to yet more waste elements and a poorer yield from sales. Thus a defect in an internal IT process (something slowing the website) causes waste in every single channel in the company.

COACHING SESSION 73

IT operations and waste

Identify five examples in your IT operation that impact part of or the entire organization.

1. _____

_____

_____

_____

2. _____

_____

_____

_____

3. _____

_____

_____

_____

4. _____

_____

_____

_____

5. _____

_____

_____

_____

Lean enterprises

These work to precisely define value in terms of specific products with identified capabilities offered at set prices through a dialogue with their customers. The process involves learning to adopt and employ a series of tools and techniques to achieve incremental improvements in an organization. Above all, Lean Thinking methods are inclusive of all employees and involve a major change in the embedded attitudes of the individuals that make up the organizations. For example:

- **Value Stream Mapping** A technique used to identify material and information flow through a supply chain or through a sequence of activities. Non-value-added time stands out in Value Stream Mapping, thus providing a clear view of opportunities for process improvement and transformation.

- **Value Stream Map** The transformed end-to-end process.

- **Action Plan** This describes how and when improvements are realized through the application of hybridized lean problem-solving tools. Over time, the steps in the Action Plan become the basis for continuous process improvements.

Kaizen and kanban

Kaizen and kanban are lean tools used to change the way the product is produced. They are used to eliminate the waste in the products being produced. The main goal is to create a 'better' process by solving problems on a continual basis.

Kaizen is a Japanese business philosophy focused on making constant improvements. Kaizen means 'change for the better'. Its underlying concept stresses that there will always be room for improvement; fundamentally, kaizen aims to improve all activities and processes and eliminate waste and excess. Perhaps the most surprising and impressive thing about undertaking a lean journey is how quickly change can be effected. A palpable shift in attitudes of people towards their work and workplace can be evident within weeks.

At the core of **kanban** are three principles:

1. **Visualizing the workflow** Split the work into pieces, write each item on a card and put it on the wall. Label columns to illustrate where each item is in the workflow.

2. **Limiting Work in Progress (WIP)** Assign explicit limits to how many items may be in progress at each workflow state.

3. **Measuring the lead time** (The lead time is the average time it takes to complete one item, sometimes called the 'cycle time'.) Optimize the process to make lead time as small and predictable as possible.

COACHING SESSION 74

Lean Thinking and your organization

What applications of Lean Thinking relate to current operations in your organization and how might it be used to improve them? Consider five examples.

1. _____

_____

_____

_____

_____

2. _____

_____

_____

_____

_____

3. _____

_____

_____

_____

_____

4. _____

_____

_____

_____

_____

5. _____

_____

_____

_____

_____

NEXT STEPS

This chapter set out to stimulate thinking about new methods and to question amalgamated approaches. It contrasted and compared traditional and agile development methods, and briefly described Lean Thinking methods and tools which you might consider using for your own organization.

This completes the serious subject matter – the following chapter looks at why having fun in a project aids productivity.

👍 TAKEAWAYS

Apply the Seven Wastes to your current flow of work. What impediments exist to adding value and which steps are nugatory?

_____

_____

_____

_____

_____

_____

_____

_____

_____

_____

What necessary changes have you identified by reflecting on your own project's purpose and development processes?

_____

_____

_____

_____

_____

_____

_____

_____

_____

_____

_____

What arguments will you put forward for changes to your organization's way of producing products, services and business results?

_____

_____

_____

_____

_____

_____

_____

_____

_____

_____

What changes can you identify to the way you collect feedback on your products or services?

_____

_____

_____

_____

_____

_____

_____

_____

_____

_____

_____

_____

_____

_____

THE USE OF HUMOUR AND FUN AT WORK

12

 OUTCOMES FROM THIS CHAPTER

- Understand why having fun at work is important in both the general work and temporary project management contexts.
- Assess how you, the team and your organization shapes up.
- Make work fun and productive as a team member and a boss.
- Know that humour can be a doubled-edged sword.

Work is a justifiably serious business but that doesn't mean you can't have fun, too. Having fun with work colleagues is not new; it's become more of a characteristic of efficient workplaces than it might have been in the past. Certainly, since the arrival of the dot.com bubble it is an integral part of the modern business ethos to refresh people's brains and bond teams together. Research has indicated that having fun in the workplace enhances employee engagement. Actively engaged employees bring discretionary effort to work in addition to their normal contribution; they are loyal and productive and, as a consequence, create sustainable client relationships whereby organizations become more profitable.

WHY HAVING FUN AT WORK IS IMPORTANT

'All work and no play make Jack a dull boy.'

In a pressured project management environment, it's even more important that your people really enjoy what they're doing. Why? Because many of them may well be working on your project as well as being involved in 'business as usual', so they'll need all the resilience and commitment they can lay their hands on.

Building a fun and happy working environment will help them and you to ensure that your people enjoy the experience of being on a project, a vital aspect without which PMs are unlikely to succeed. An unexpected sign of your success at team building in a fun working environment is when people dread the end of the project as team members are reassigned or return to their full-time role.

During her research for a doctoral dissertation in management, Erin Fluegge Woolf discovered that, 'With people spending more and more of their lives at work, they feel they might as well make it enjoyable, and our study finds surprising payoffs when they do.' She goes on to say: 'Not only did employees report being in better moods and more engaged in their work, they also performed better on the job.' Fluegge Woolf is not alone as Hemsath and Yersk have gone so far as to suggest that having fun at work might be the single most important factor in organizational effectiveness and success.

COMPARISON OF A HAPPY AND AN UNHAPPY SCENARIO

With so much on your mind as a PM, you might wonder if you really need to spend valuable time and scarce resources on developing a fun environment for your people. Let's imagine that you have decided to do just that. So what can you expect?

Having fun at work is likely to engender a healthy working environment in which people...

- are really engaged with what they do, so they do their best
- have strong working relationships across the hierarchy
- are more innovative and creative
- are more focused, more willing and more professional
- perhaps most importantly, will be ambassadors for the change and make it happen.

COACHING SESSION 75

Self-assessment: happiness/unhappiness in the workplace

Think about a time when you were really happy at work. Work through the following tables making notes as you progress.

Describe the overarching organizational culture.	

Describe the situation in which you were operating.	
Note what features of the situation made you happy.	
How did your happiness make you feel?	
What impact did these feelings have on you personally?	
How did others perceive you?	
What impact did how you felt have on others?	

What was the single most impactful outcome of your happiness?	

Now think about a time when you were consistently unhappy at work. Work through the table making notes as you progress.

Describe the overarching organizational culture.	
Describe the situation in which you were operating.	
Note what features of the situation made you unhappy.	
How did your unhappiness make you feel?	

What impact did these feelings have on you personally?	
How did others perceive you?	
What impact did how you felt have on others?	
What was the single most impactful outcome of your unhappiness?	

Now compare these two situations where you were really happy and unhappy. Record below anything you have learned from this exercise that will help you to justify to your sponsor the importance of developing a fun project environment.

ASSESSING HOW YOUR EXISTING TEAM AND ORGANIZATION SHAPES UP

In this section we will examine how you can develop a strategy for using appropriate humour and fun in the workplace, improving your project team's experience while moulding it to what can be afforded.

COACHING SESSION 76

Assessment: fun in your current workplace

Consider your current workplace:

Describe the attitude of senior management to making it a fun place to work.	
How do you feel about that?	
How do you think your colleagues feel about it?	
What could the senior management team do better?	

What could they do more of?	
What should they do less of?	
What 'happiness' benefits would accrue from these measures being taken?	
What commercial benefits would accrue?	

You've looked at people's attitudes to fun at work, so let's look now at what options are available for engendering an atmosphere of working hard and having fun too.

COACHING SESSION 77

Fun ideas

There are very many ways to introduce fun into workplaces; some involve a cost to the organization, others will be cost-free. Look at the list of ideas which follows and indicate whether it's something you'd like to see in your project team. Decide whether you think it's feasible or not and give it a score of 1–10 (where 10 is high), to indicate how strongly you feel about including it. The list is not exhaustive so add your own ideas, too.

Activity	Feasible ☑ or Not feasible ☒	Score
Book club		
Chill-out areas/water cooler areas		
Company band/pop group		
Cooking/dining club		
Daily team meetings		
Days out to the RHS Chelsea, Derby, Royal Ascot, Cheltenham Races, the Grand National, Formula One at Silverstone, Cup Final, etc.		
Discount purchase club		
'Employee of the Month'		
Fitness centre or external fitness club membership		
Merchandise club		
Movie or video club		
Pub quiz evenings		
Social club		
Sports club (internal or external with membership)		
Staff sports reams		
Staff squash/tennis ladder		
Subsidized staff canteen/café		
Team night out at the pub		

Theatre/concert trips		
Other:		

Now record below what you have learned from all of the coaching sessions in this chapter in terms of creating a fun working environment.

_____

_____

_____

_____

_____

_____

_____

_____

_____

_____

_____

HUMOUR AS A PUT-DOWN

Humour can be a double-edged sword. It is sometimes used by predatory individuals to isolate, intimidate or humiliate people, especially those exhibiting superior performance, status or relationships. Use of humour which puts people down or reduces their credibility in a group situation is a passive-aggressive behaviour; it is prevalent in some cultures but it is not acceptable in the team structure of a project.

COACH'S TIP

Use humour in moderation

There is nothing wrong with being witty about what you are doing on a project as long as you're not breaking the team spirit or spoiling the brand associated with what you're delivering. An excessive or satirical use of humour may be a sign to you as PM that you need to spend more one-to-one time with team members and give them the opportunity for two-way feedback.

CONCLUSION

I hope that readers will have experienced mourning their team members as the project ends because this is a sign that the team gelled and was successful. I have friends collected over several decades through working well together under extreme pressure or in poor work environments. It can be a very bonding experience.

PMs need to get the balance right between work and play, humour and being serious, having fun and plain, hard graft. Having the right balance will support you through the inevitable tough periods. People will recognize your efforts to inject a sense of fun, achieve commitment and encourage collaboration rather than competition in order to celebrate the rich diversity within the team.

TAKEAWAYS

What evidence is there that having fun at work is important and useful?

_____

_____

_____

_____

_____

_____

_____

_____

_____

_____

How would you present to your sponsor the results of assessing yourself, your team and the organization in terms of fun adding business value?

_____

_____

_____

_____

_____

_____

_____

_____

_____

_____

_____

_____

What action plan do you have for introducing more measures for fun to aid increased productivity?

_____

_____

_____

_____

_____

_____

_____

_____

_____

_____

_____

_____

_____

_____

_____

_____

ACTION PLAN

You now need to conclude your learning and decide development priorities. You were asked in the introductory chapter to consider studying the material at a number of levels to make full use of the capability in your current day-to-day work:

- Are we doing things right?

- Are we doing the right things?

- How do we know what is right for us?

This first question implies that there is a method, model, best practice or technique which acts as a benchmark for comparison in terms of what you're doing versus what is considered optimal.

So, using Chapter 1 as an example, you are given four theories of motivation to absorb, contrast, compare and apply to your own work. You are also given a checklist for aspects that employers value in employees and questionnaires to assess your own self-motivation and to assess your team members' ability to be self-motivated.

Applying the second question here may lead you to feel that you have gaps in your policies, procedures and ways of working that lead to team members being demotivated or requiring an intervention to improve performance. The project environment may need to be enhanced to improve the climate at work and to raise morale.

Last but not least, applying the third question invites you to think more extrinsically, strategically and systemically. In the case of motivation, this may be to look at the expectations set for employees by the company, its customers and supply chain. Equally, the whole performance measurement system applied to change agents possibly within your sector or industry might be worth evaluating or benchmarking.

COACHING SESSION 78

A final task...

Apply this triple-loop learning logic to each of the subjects and themes illustrated in the following table. Ask yourself and answer each of the three questions applied to each theme – both to consolidate your learning and also to shape what you are going to do next.

Make mind maps or charts or create structured notes to help you commit the theory to memory and to emphasize the material that is the *most relevant* to your current project.

It is important that you decide how you are going to apply theory to everyday practice and to prioritize each activity in terms of urgency and importance.

What can you do first that will give you the most benefit and reduce risks or issues facing you?

Chapter subject	Themes	
Motivated project team	• Applying motivational theory	• Assessing team members
PM as effective influencer	• Balanced push and pull	• Matches strategy and stakeholder
Proactively resolves conflict	• Understanding emotional roots • Addressing confrontation	• Predicting and preventing conflict
End-to-end communications	• Understanding the mission	• Managing the messages
Political savvy	• Sources of power	• Politically intelligent PM
Stakeholder management	• Analysis and evaluation • Engaging stakeholders	• Using intelligence collected
Mobilizing change	• Understanding change	• Creating impetus
Collaborative relationships	• Relationship tips	• Use of sponsor
Helping the customer journey	• The right investment	• Thinking creatively
'Lean' and 'agile' approaches	• Contrast and compare	• Balancing value and risk
Making work fun and productive	• Productive and happy team	• Organizational effectiveness

Don't forget that there are materials to download as explained at the beginning of this workbook as well as a downloadable list of reference materials which provide you with opportunity to gain further knowledge and insight. Only you can maximize the value by contextualizing the workbook content to your role, project and organization. Remember that having fun works, too!

QUICK HELP SHEET

The following flowchart illustrates the chapter-by-chapter coverage and the two or three main themes covered.

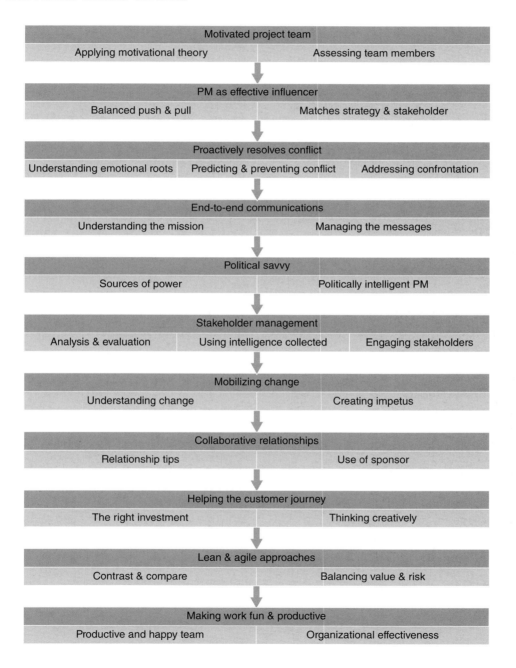

INDEX

The author and publisher would like to thank the following for permission to reproduce figures used in this book: Belbin Associates (Figure 4.3: Team Role Summary Descriptions); Cole-McKee Partnership/Hudson Associates (Figure 2.2: Productive behaviours in personal power and Figure 2.6: Positive influence process)